Compensating Non-Supervisory
Professional Employees

Research for Business Decisions, No. 8

Other Titles in This Series

Compensating Non-Supervisory Professional Employees

by
John W. Crim

RESEARCH PRESS

Library of Congress Cataloging in Publication Data

Crim, John Winthrop, 1924-
    Compensating non-supervisory professional
employees.

    (Research for business decisions ; no. 8)
    Bibliography: p.
    Includes index.
    1. Professions—Salaries, pensions, etc.—United States.
2. Middle managers—Salaries, pensions, etc.—United
States. 3. Compensation management—United States.
I. Title. II. Series.

HD4965.U5C74 1978 331.2'81'658400973   78-24418
ISBN 0-8357-0964-7
ISBN 0-8357-0965-5 pbk.

PREFACE

The exchange of value between employer and employee appears to have been a key consideration in the operation of commercial enterprises since the beginning of recorded history. The Holy Bible, in Mathew, Chapter 20, tells us of the disagreement between a vineyard owner and his employees regarding the wages they earned for the hours they worked.

The subject of appropriate compensation has fascinated me through twenty years as an industrial engineer and manager, and eight subsequent years teaching Wage and Salary Administration to university students. It is my sincere hope that this research will provide at least a stepping-stone toward our understanding and application of compensation methods; particularly in that "never never land" of evaluating the compensation of a "manager" versus the "professional individual contributor."

My special appreciation goes to my dissertation committee chairman, Dr. Harding Young and my committee members, Drs. Michael Mescon, Donald Crane, and Richard Henderson for their confidence, patience, and assistance.

Well over one hundred practitioners of compensation devoted as much as several hours each, to supplying the data for this study. For this I shall be forever grateful to each and every one of them. Among those I especially wish to thank are Arthur Ring, John Cesinger, John Mueller, James Moore, George Foote, Don Winton, and P.A. VanWagenen who gave so generously of their counsel.

The research assistance of Betty McMurtry was invaluable and Sharon Harper's typing was a cheerful display of continual fast turnarounds. My daughters, Lucinda and Martha volunteered many hours of searching the library for elusive reference material. My deepest gratitude goes to Susie Crim who materially helped to make this work possible, and to my dear wife, Jeanie, who bore far more than her share of the worry which so often seems to accompany any worthwhile endeavor.

CONTENTS

TABLES

FIGURES

CHAPTER 1

THE STUDY

Background

The compensation literature appears to present no specific model for an integrated compensation system to be used by a private enterprise operating in the free economy of our American democracy. As a starting point in attempting to construct such a model, we might hazard the generalization that, under the competitive conditions of free enterprise, each company seeks to optimize the long-run economic value received from each employee in return for the compensation paid to that employee.

The many "means, channels, or factors" through which employers pay their employees have been treated at length. Belcher lists 113 "selected fringe benefits" in *addition* to wages and salaries, through which employers pay employees. These benefits run the gamut from holidays, Christmas bonuses, and health insurance, to such personnel services as cafeterias, beauty parlors, and income tax counseling.[1] All are ways in which employees receive their total compensation package.

Much has also been written about "what it *is* that motivates an employee." An important part of the "behavioral" approach to Management is its focus upon the myriad devices used by employers to induce the employee to produce the greatest value for his organization. Many of these devices can be included in the board term "compensation."

The Conference Board (formerly the National Industrial Conference Board), the Bureau of Labor Statistics, and the American Management Association are three of a number of organizations which maintain continuing surveys of actual compensation paid to employees in *specific jobs* throughout industry.

However, little seems to have been published from a "systems approach" to the strategy and planning by which a company fits together the many pieces into a single integrated compensation package for *all* its employees from a company viewpoint. Such an approach would address itself to such questions as: How much total compensation can (or should) a company pay to each of its employee groups for the work they do for the company? What should be the grand total of compensation for all groups? How can each factor of compensation be tailored, company-wide, to achieve the greatest motivation for the lowest company expenditure?

In the case of compensation for unionized non-exempt employees, it might be assumed that the strategy is largely one of out-maneuvering the union, in a defensive manner, to minimize total compensation cost. If this were a company's strategy, presumably it would been chosen in preference to their taking an aggressive, creative, constructive approach to compensation design. On the other hand, in the case of exempt employees, who at the present writing are predominantly non-union, a constructive model of compensation might seem quite appropriate and useful.

Problem

In order to construct such an overall, company-wide, ideal compensation model, one particular area seems to call for special attention. This is the fine line discriminating the "manager" from the "professional."

In the classic private industrial enterprise in this country, the "manager of people" is presumably motivated by the possibility of obtaining a desirable compensation package which will include: salary, deferred benefits, fringe benefits, bonuses, "prestige and status;" all theoretically related to the performance of the people he manages and, therefore, indirectly related to his own performance as a manager. How is the "professional" to be comparably compensated when he has no subordinates to manage, and when it is difficult, or even impossible, to measure his personal performance? How does a company design a compensation package which will motivate the professional in the same way as it motivates a manager?

David Belcher refers to the distinction between the compensation of the two groups as the "Double-Track or Parellel-ladder" system of compensation adding:

> . . .professionals can advance in salary and organization status without becoming managers. Although the similar complexities in salary determination of the two groups do argue for integration, organizations would be wise to question whether the two groups want to make and be paid for the same contributions. Present limited knowledge suggests that middle managers, and some professionals, want to be paid for job contributions (given that they have some voice in designing the job around their attributes). However, most professionals expect to be paid for *personal contributions* without respect to job assignment. To the extent that this picture is correct, integration would seem to make salaries for both groups more a reward for personal contributions than job contributions. Our model of the employment exchange would suggest separate treatment for the two groups.[2]

It is the "Double-Track System of Progression" upon which the writer proposes focusing the research of the present dissertation.

The Fair Labor Standards Act of 1938, in discriminating between those employees subject to the act, and those not subject to its requirements (particularly in regard to overtime pay provisions), has defined the "exempt employee" as being either "Executive, Administrative, or Professional." Accepting the classical and universal definition of the functions of a manager as: Plan, Organize, Direct, and Control indicates that only the "executive" qualifies as a manager. Neither the "administrator" nor the "professional" is required to supervise (direct) any other person, while the "executive" must direct the work of at least two other employees.

On the other hand, the "executive" is not required to have "advanced knowledge in a field of science or learning acquired by a prolonged course of specialized intellectual instruction and study," which is the special requirement of a "professional."[3]

Thus, in simplest terms, we have:

a.) A "manager" whose major responsibilities entail the supervision of people, but who may or may not, as a secondary qualification, also have specialized training of a scientific or intellectual nature.

b.) A "professional" who must have the above specialized education but whose major duties do not entail the supervision of people.

Traditonally, the compensation level of a manager in this country appears to have been related loosely to some criterion such as "profit responsibility" or "responsibility over other people." It is almost axiomatic that the "superior receives greater compensation than his subordinate." However, no such criterion seems applicable to the "professional" who has no subordinates, and whose work by its very nature, is usually related to profit in only the most indirect or remote manner.

Our American industrial society seems instinctively to recognnize a logical direct correlation between "prestige" and "compensation level." The "prestige," in turn, is often related to "the number of people over whom one is the boss." Hence, the more people the manager bosses, the more compensation he can expect to command.

Our American society also recognizes the contributions of medical doctors, lawyers, dentists, and similar professionals who frequently work as independent practitioners and whose work usually entails a minimum of supervision over other people. It is easy for society to relate the compensation of these independent professionals to the *need* for their particular learned expertise. However, when we place the manager and the professional together in a single organization (both as employees), we seem to lose our comparative reference for lack of a common denominator. It is the writer's intuitive suggestion that in the face of this dilemma, organizations instinctively gravitate to "supervisory power" as a basis for comparative compensation, rather than to the relative "need for the expertise." This is probably caused by the fact that the former is usually much easier to define and measure than the latter.

The "Double-Track system of progression" suggests that there *is* a common denominator by which to measure relative compensation received by the manager and by the professional.

Importance Of The Study

It has been authoritatively stated that "On a national scale compensation costs constitute upwards of 70% of the total costs of a (manufactured) product."[4] This proportion is even higher in the service industries than in the manufacturing sector. It is, therefore, axiomatical that the largest single item of outgoing cash flow, in most profit-making enterprises, is "payroll" or, more correctly, "total compensation." Thus the leverage or efficiency-of-return on money spent on compensation can exert a greater effect upon company profits than can the control of any other item of expense. It pragmatically follows that one of the major business concerns of any company management is the careful design and control of the compensation package.

The difference between the compensation of the non-exempt group and the exempt group is that the per-employee cost of the exempt group is the greater, and has drawn the attention of this present study.

Another relevant point is that since 1955 white-collar employees in this country have exceeded the total number of blue-collar employees, and the numerical difference is continually widening.[5] This trend indicates that the ratio of exempt employees to the total labor force may continually rise, thus emphasizing the ever-increasing importance of controlling the cost of the exempt employees.

The exempt employee group is composed largely of "managers" and "professionals," as previously defined. Together, managers and professionals constitute an exceptionally important and sensitive collection of employees who stand at the "elite" end of the spectrum of all employees in an industrial organization.

The important point is that the managers and professionals *are* often "together" or similar in educational and social backgrounds. As previously noted, some managers might also qualify as "professionals" as well as managers. Professionals have invested a considerable portion of their lifetimes in preparation for their professions. They are presumably valuable to their firm *as professionals*, yet they work in an environment which might easily attract them out of the "professional" and into the "manager" group. It is apparent that any firm should seek to have both groups motivated to maximum performance by the compensation and promotion ladders available to them; and each ladder must provide both challenge and satisfaction to the employee.

It, therefore, becomes increasingly incumbent upon industry to prepare to integrate compensation of "professionals" and "managers" in some valid manner which will prevent the dysfunctional effects upon the organization which could result when "professionals" yield to the attraction to "cross-over" to the "manager" group.

NOTES

[1]David Belcher, *Compensation Administration* (Englewood Cliffs: Prentice Hall, 1974), pp. 364-365.

[2]Op. cit., Belcher, p. 541.

[3]Op. cit., p. 433.

[4]H.G. Zollitsch and A. Langsner, *Wage and Salary Administration*, 2nd ed. (Cincinnati: South-Western Publishing Company, 1970), p. 10.

[5]Ibid., p. 17.

CHAPTER 2

DESIGN OF THE STUDY

Objectives

The objectives of this dissertation are to:

1. *Investigate* the extent to which American industrial firms have, as of today, adopted "Double-Track" systems of compensation administration.

2. *Describe* and *compare* the characteristics of double-track systems now in operation in this country.

3. *Predict* the trend of future installation of double-track systems in American industry.

4. As a means to the above ends, current American authorities on exempt compensation will be identified through the survey. Further inquiries and interviews with these authorities will influence the final conclusions.

Definitions And Terminology

Total Compensation

All forms of payment received by an employee from his employer. For purposes of this paper, these shall fall into the following two broad categories:

    a. Financial or economic; such as salary, bonus, incentive premiums, overtime pay, vacation, payments in kind, personnel services, economic security, and any factor with an assignable dollar value to the employee representing a cost to the employer.

    b. Psychological or non-financial; psychic income such as self-actualization, satisfaction, or well-being in the mind of the employee. This includes status; prestige; position; physical environment; awards; acclaim; the right to exercise authority over other people, things, or concepts, the opportunity to do original thinking and to take action of a creative nature.

Employee

Any person fulfilling an agreement with another party (the employer) by which the employee regularly provides a service of economic value to the employer while the employer retains:

  a. The right to control and direct the employee's actions.
  b. The obligation to compensate the employee for his service on a bilaterally predetermined basis.

Employer

The second party in the above definition.

Exempt Employee

One who must regularly exercise discretion and independent judgement in his work, and who devotes at least 80% of his time to duties in at least one of these three categories:

Executive

Primary duties are the management of the enterprise. Must direct the work of at least two other employees, must have authority (or recommendation influence) hiring, firing, or status-changing of other employees. Must have a salary of at least $125 per week.

Administrative

Primary duties are office of non-manual work related to policies or general business operations, or must directly assist a proprietor, executive or administrator in such duties. Must earn a salary or fees of at least $125 per week.

Professional

Primary duties require advanced knowledge in a field of science or learning acquired by a prolonged course of specialized intellectual instruction and study. Work must be original, creative, intellectual and varied, and must command a salary or fee of at least $140 per week. (This category is intended to consist largely of scientists, and licensed practitioners of

medicine, law, engineering, and accounting who are neither
"executives" nor "administrators.")[1]

Double-Track System of Progression and Compensation

A distinct framework within the formal compensation policy of a
given organization whereby at least two general tracks of
ascending compensation steps are available to exempt employees:
(1) A "managerial" track to be ascended through increasing
responsibility for supervision or direction of people, and (2) A
"professional" track to be ascended through increasing
contributions of a professional nature which do *not* mainly entail
the supervision or direction of people.

Reward

A payment to an employee, usually for above-average
performance.   The value of the payment is unilaterally
determined by the payor.   (This should not be confused with
other forms of compensation which are bilaterally determined.)

Labor Market

The sum total of all available persons ready, willing and able to
be productively employed in the United States.   (Includes both
exempt and non-exempt people.)

Motivation

Any influence that causes an individual consciously to select a
course of action for himself other than one he might have chosen
in the absence of that influence.[2]

Satisfaction

Subjective feelings of relief or pleasure which can be reported by
the person who experiences them, but which cannot be observed
directly by anyone else.[3]

Methodology

I.

A "state-of-the-art" survey was made to appraise the current existence of "Double-Track compensation and progression systems" in American industrial firms.

The membership list of the American Compensation Association (with national offices at 1910 Cochran Road, Pittsburgh, Pennsylvania) was felt to be an appropriate and representative total population for such a survey. The A.C.A. has more than 2,500 members employed by organizations representing industry, finance, transportation, utilities, consulting, education, and government throughout the United States and Canada. All members are directly involved with compensation administration, at the policy and/or implementation level, within their firms or for clients.

The frame of respondents to be surveyed by mail was derived from the A.C.A. membership list as follows:

1. On the rationale that there is a direct correlation between the size of the firm and the probability of existence of a double-track system in the company, the A.C.A. membership list was reduced to those members employed by the largest 400 American industrial corporations (in sales) as designated by *Fortune* magazine.

2. To eliminate duplications of mailings to firms having more than one employee in A.C.A., only the one employee from each firm who had the most appropriate-appearing title for our purposes was retained on the list. (e.g. "Director of Compensation" would be chosen in preference to "Director of Labor Relations," "Wage & Salary Analyst," or "Personnel Manager.") In most cases, this selection was a subjective judgement, but it was felt that if two members of a given firm found that they had received identical questionnaires concerning their company's policies, the probability of a response from either one would be greatly reduced.

The above steps generated a list of about 250 names, which was the frame of respondents.

The questionnaire, with cover letter, follows:

AMERICAN COMPENSATION ASSOCIATION

Suite 660 Manor Oak One   1910 Cochran Road   Pittsburgh, Pennsylvania 15220
Telephone 412-343-5477

Officers of ACA have agreed to cooperate with Professor John W. Crim of Auburn University in a survey for a doctoral dissertation project which is being directed by a committee of four professors on the faculty of the Department of Management, School of Business Administration, Georgia State University.

The attached brief questionnaire, which is being mailed to a limited number of selected ACA members, was designed by Professor Crim and his committee. It is suggested that you fill in the answers as completely as possible and return the completed questionnaire to Professor Crim, whose address is on the last page of the questionnaire, within the next 10 days if possible. All respondents will receive a report of the ultimate findings of the survey.

No names of persons or companies will be used in the final report without specific permission.

Sincerely,

Arthur D. Ring
Executive Director

ADR:ds
attachment

SURVEY OF COMPENSATION AND PROGRESSION LADDERS FOR MANAGERS AND PROFESSIONALS

In answering the first ten questions, please assume the following definitions for "manager" and "professional," regardless of your company's specific interpretation of the terms:

<u>Manager</u>: An employee whose major duties entail directing the work of subordinates. This term includes foremen, supervisors, department heads, etc., up through and including the chief executive. Though a "manager" may also possess the training and intellectual qualifications of a "professional," his major duties involve the management of people and their work.

<u>Professional</u>: An employee who devotes very little time to directing the work of other people, but whose work regularly entails non-routine duties requiring originality, discretion, independent judgment, creativity and analysis; who holds a minimum of a four-year college degree (frequently more), in a specialized area of science, engineering, accounting, finance, medicine, law, psychology, etc. A certification or license-to-practice is often implied.

Your company name:_____

Your name and title:_____

1. Total number of "managers" in your company. (Your considered estimate is sufficient if specific data is unavailable):_____

2. Total number of "professionals" in your company. (Again, your estimate is acceptable): _____

3. Total number of employees in your company, <u>including</u> those in question 1 and 2, above:_____

4. Does your company policy clearly distinguish at least two separate compensation and progression ladders for managers and professionals?:

Yes_____
No_____

Your comments, please:

5. IMPORTANT: If the above answer is "yes", and your company has a standard written explanation by which your employees are advised of these separate ladders (such as a Personnel or Policy Manual) would you be good enough to send us a copy along with this questionnaire?

6. Does the "professional" in your firm have the possibility of reaching a compensation level which is <u>second only</u> to that of your Chief Executive?

Yes_____
No_____

a. If "No", how high <u>does</u> the professional ladder go compared to that of your Chief Executive?

b. Has any "professional" in your firm ever reached that level which is second only to that of your Chief Executive?

Yes_____
No_____

7. If your company does not distinguish between at least two separate compensation and progression ladders for managers and professionals, do you think your company will be doing so within the next few years?

Yes_____
No_____

Your comments:

8. Based upon your personal experience, please give the name of any person, anywhere in America, whom you consider to be an authority on the subject of compensating managers and professionals:

9. Please give the name of one or more companies which you know to have had experience in the application of a formal framework of comparative compensation of the two groups:

10. Additional comments. Please add any observations, suggestions, or reasons for your answers etc., which may occur to you. Add another page of paper if necessary. Your comments are sincerely solicited and will form an important part of the analysis of this questionnaire.:

II.   As indicated in question #5 in the questionnaire, written descriptions of existing double-track systems were obtained from all respondents who would make them available to us. These were compared in detail for characteristics, breadth, scope, trends, and compensation factors.

III.   Special attention was taken of all "authorities" suggested by question #8 in the questionnaire. Some 35 personal interviews were arranged with respondents and consultants whenever additional information, clarification, enlargement, or individual opinions were deemed appropriate. These interviews were made by the writer, either in person or by telephone.

IV.   A suggested model of a Double-Track system was constructed for a hypothetical American industrial firm. This model was generally structured according to current practice of American firms, but was designed with a view of future industrial needs as elicited from results of the survey.

NOTES

[1]Defined by the Fair Labor Standards Act of 1938.

[2]S. W. Gellerman, *Management by Motivation* (New York: American Management Association, 1968), p. 171.

[3]Ibid., p. 172.

CHAPTER 3

OVERVIEW OF COMPENSATION

Model Of Compensation Theories And Influences

The model on the following page was originated by the writer. It was initially drawn to assist the writer in arranging and understanding in his own mind the interrelationships effecting the setting of compensation levels. The model was then used as a format by which to describe the theories and influences in a logical sequence on the following pages. It is included here, in the hope that it will help convey the clearest picture of the concepts subsequently described.

At the top of the model, the "Social" wage theories are those which seem, intuitively, to have least effect upon the wage levels in a democracy. Coming down the page through the "funnel" are the theories which more and more seem to have stronger influence upon wage levels; the closer the theory's position to "compensation" (at the bottom of the page), the more influence the theory seems to enjoy.

At the bottom of the model, the "influences" on either side of "compensation" are shown as a "balance of forces" diagram, indicating which influences tend to raise the level of compensation and which tend to drive it down.

A Conceptual Model Of The Theories Of Compensation

I.   The "Social" Wage Theories (classical). These theories, though often classified as the "classical" wage theories, are designated here as "Social" wage theories since, in every case, they attempt to explain what society "ought to pay" to one of its members, based upon the need or the "right" of that member. In no case do these theories mention, or appear to consider, the talents of the individual or the quality or quantity of work produced by that individual.

        a.   The Subsistence theory of wages: The Subsistence theory, proposed by David Ricardo about 1817, and based upon the writings of Thomas Num and Thomas R. Malthus' theory of population suggests that each member of society be provided enough food, clothing, and shelter to continue to exist.[1] The theory further implies, with some degree of naivete, that when the worker's income exceeds that subsistence level, he responds by further procreation, thus increasing the labor force and consequently lowering wages as a result of supply-and-demand.

FIGURE I

MODEL OF COMPENSATION THEORIES AND INFLUENCES

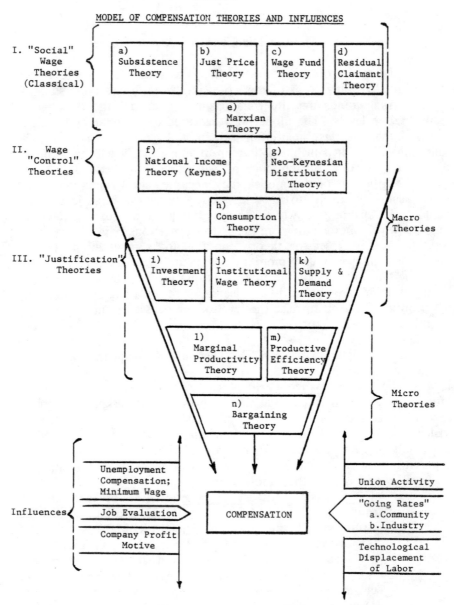

b. The Just Price theory: The Just Price theory, originally proposed by Plato and Aristotle some 300 years before Christ, suggests that each person born into the world is foreordained to occupy exactly the same status and to enjoy the same creature comforts as did his parents before him.[2] Therefore, society owes that individual sufficient compensation to maintain exactly the same position of life into which he was born. The theory further suggests that the price of any article should be just sufficient, but no more than sufficient, to cover the cost of production which, in turn, is based upon the accustomed standards of living of the producers of that item.[3] By inference, this theory has no provisions of entrepreneureal profit and makes no recognition of differences in productive efficiency between two workers.

c. The Wage Fund theory: The Wage Fund theory, advanced by John Stuart Mill in the 1830's, suggests that the wages of an employee are paid from a fund which presumably has been accumulated by the entrepreneur from his operations of previous years.[4] This fund which, to some extent, was under the control of the entrepreneur, was then divided evenly between all employees. The theory has some obvious shortcomings if we assume, as is usually the case in a profit making organization, that wages are paid essentially from current business operations rather than from past operations. However, the theory does seem to possess some validity when applied to not-for-profit organizations such as government and public service whereby the wage fund is actually forecasted and drawn from tax monies.

d. The Residual Claimant theory: In the late nineteenth century, Francis A. Walker proposed a version of the Wage Fund theory whereby he hypothesized that the wage fund derived not from previous years' operations, but simply from the residue of total revenues after all other legitimate expenses of business operations such as rent, taxes, interest, profits, etc., had been deducted.[5] Following this through to its logical conclusion we could find that if the "other expenses" consumed all of revenue, labor would receive no wages whatsoever.

e. Marxian theory: Karl Marx's wage theory is essentially the inversion of the "Residual Claimant" theory, inasmuch as he suggests that labor is the sole source of economic value and that therefore labor should exercise the prime claim on revenue.[6] This premise would indicate that the price of an article should consist solely of labor value, and that any other value collected by the entrepreneur represents unacceptable exploitation of labor. Marx further suggests that the displacement of labor, through technological progress, is disfunctional to the system and would eventually destroy capitalism. The Marxian theory would appear to be the ideological basis upon which certain segments of the labor union movement militantly oppose automation.

II.   The Wage "Control" Theories. These theories suggest that, somewhere between the extremes of a pure dictatorship and a pure democracy, there is room for a mode of government which frankly and openly permits, even demands, some degree of indirect control of wage levels.

> f.   The National Income theory: John Maynard Keynes, the spokesman for the National Income theory (sometimes called the "Full Employment Wage Theory")[7] hypothesizes that full employment is a function of national income. National income, in turn, is equal to the total of consumption plus private and public investment. If the national income falls below a level which produces full employment, it is then the responsibility of the federal government to manipulate one of the three variables so as to cause national income to rise again to a point where full employment is achieved. Keynes suggests that government is the one agent powerful enough to control monetary and fiscal policies, as well as to enforce direct edicts upon private enterprise, such that full employment is maintained and, indirectly, the desired wage level is upheld. National Income theory appears to treat the labor supply as though it were fixed. In actuality, though growing, the national labor force varies within rather wide limits. This short-term variation is a result of the fact that a substantial segment of the population can, in the short run, decide whether they are actually a part of the labor force. This personal redundant choice can be exercised by a "second wage-earner in the family," by teenagers who have not previously been in the labor force, by older people who may be able to choose whether to be employed or by recipients of unemployment compensation who, for the short term, may actually not be available for alternate employment. Thus the critics of the National Income theory suggest that a fault

of the theory lies in its failure to recognize this fluctuating labor force.

g. Neo-Keynesian Distribution theory: The Neo-Keynesian Distribution theory is a refinement or extension of the National Income theory, in that it attempts to explain how full employment conditions can be achieved without conflicting with general living standards or with stable prices.[8] This theory is, therefore, actually a theory of the general wage level on both the long and short term. The theory also recognizes that the general level of wages, in the short run, is determined by bargaining between the capitalist and the employee. The Distribution theory is a departure from the theories previously mentioned in which economic forces *alone* determine the wage level. Thus the ever-changing labor supply is given some consideration in this theory.

h. The Consumption theory: The Consumption theory, sometimes referred to as the "purchasing power" theory, is generally credited to Henry Ford who, in 1915, unilaterally instituted the $5-a-day wage in his factories. That rate was generally considered in competing automobiles plants to be about twice the normal wage.[9] Those who defend Mr. Ford's action as a "new wage theory" suggest that high money wages encourage consumption, increase demand for products, and thereby lower commodity prices. This theory is included in "Wage Control Theories" since, indeed, it involves a macro approach to the general wage level throughout the entire economy. However, the instrument of control is the private enterprise itself, rather than the federal government.

III. The "Justification" theories These theories are so labeled because their authors apparently attempt to explain or "justify" the reasons for an individual worker's compensation level. The first three theories approach the wage level from an overall macro-economic viewpoint while the remaining theories are viewed strictly from a micro-economic viewpoint.

i. The Investment theory:[10] Gitelman recognizes that labor markets vary in the scope of "worker investment" required for their particular industry. Generally, the wider the labor market the higher the wage. The individual worker's "investment" consists of the education, training, and experience which he has invested in his life's work.

Individual workers vary in their desire to maximize income, just as employing organizations vary in their worker investment requirement. Thus Gitelman hypothesizes that an individual worker's compensation is determined by the rate of return on that worker's investment. The theory conceptually combines broad economic influences on compensation with the specific means whereby a worker may control the level of his own compensation.

j.   Institutional Wage theory:[11] The Institutional Wage theory is an attempt to place the "level of compensation" on a "system" or "empirical and quantitative" basis. To include such considerations as wage experience, variability of wage relationships, latitude of decision-makers, influence of collective bargaining, etc., is to follow an inter-disciplinary approach to compensation. Proponents of the theory suggest that a wage level depends upon a variety of choices of decision-makers, and that weights can be assigned to these choices. All types of wage structures are considered, such as inter-personal, inter-firm, inter-area, inter-occupational, and inter-industry. The theory suggests that one must analyze compensation from a dynamic, continually-changing basis, rather than assuming that we can vary only one factor while holding constant all other factors affecting compensation.

k.   Supply and Demand theory:[12] A review of selected wage theories would be incomplete without reference to the classic theory of supply and demand. Probably the least refuted theory of compensation is this hypothesis that if jobs are few and supply of workers is high, then wages will fall. Conversely, if jobs are plentiful and there is a shortage of workers, wages will rise. In the long run, wages will seek a level of equilibrium where the demand curve intersects the supply curve.

The theories outlined above are essentially "macro" in nature, since each attempts in some way, to describe or account for the broad economic influences of society which effect the level of compensation of all workers. The following theories have been termed "micro" in nature since they treat the wage structure, within a given industry, or even a given company, which directly involves the bargain and the exchange between employer and employee.

l.   Marginal Productivity theory: About 1826, Johann Heinrich Von Thuren, a German economist, proposed the basis for the theory of marginal productivity.   It was developed further by Philip Henry Wickstead in England, and John Bates Clark in America. The theory gained prominence in the late nineteenth century.[13]   According to this theory, the wage paid to an employee should be equal to the extra value of productivity that the employee adds to total production.   The value of the worker's production is determined by the revenue the employer can realize from the worker's productivity. As the employer hires additional workers, a point is eventually reached at which the last worker hired produces only enough product to pay his own wages. The hiring of an additional worker would result in a revenue which did not even equal that worker's wages. The last worker is called the"marginal" employee, and the increased production attributed to him is called the "marginal productivity." The wage paid to the last marginal employee determines the wage of all workers who are doing similar work.   Though the theory has come under considerable criticism from students of compensation, it does at least represent the first formal theory embracing the principle that a worker should be paid according to the quantity and quality of work which he performs.

m.   The Productive Efficiency theory: The Productive Efficiency theory is a refinement of the Marginal Productivity theory in that each worker is provided the opportunity to increase his wages by increasing his productive efficiency. This theory provides the basis for an array of motivational tools such as incentive systems, bonuses, and profit-sharing plans. Many economists feel that because of its realistic application the productivity theory is the most constructive of recent wage theories.[14]

n.   The Bargaining Theory of Wages: The beginnings of the Bargaining theory   are found in the works of Adam Smith written in 1863.[15] However, it was described more explicitly by John Davidson in the late 1890's.[16] It is the first clear presentation of the simple principle that compensation is instigated by, and dependent upon, a bargain between an employer and an employee.   The theory further indicates that the work performed by any employee is an exchange of economic value which balances the original commitment of the employer who made the bargain. The bargaining theory is based upon the assumption that there is no single fixed wage rate for a particular kind of work. Rather, there is a *range* of possible wage rates. The upper limit of this range is determined by the highest wage the employer is able or willing to pay, and the lower limit is determined by the lowest wage for which the employee is willing to work.

In actual practice in America, the lowest minimum limit which the employee will accept is, in effect, established by the Minimum Wage Law, and/or the Unemployment Compensation to which the bargaining employee may be entitled. The Bargaining Theory remains to this day probably the most practical and valid explanation for the level of a given employee's compensation. When, and if, an employee chooses to designate a union as his bargaining agent with the employer, then this theory becomes the "Collective Bargaining theory." However, the basis of the theory remains unchanged, whether the employee personally bargains for himself, or authorizes his agent to do the bargaining on his behalf.

Significantly, in appointing a union to act as his bargaining agent, the employee must forego, to a degree, certain personal rights. As is the case with any group activity where each member must subjugate certain personal rights to the good of the whole, so the union member must relinquish his right to bargain on his own behalf for any better benefits than those enjoyed by his fellow union members.

The Influences Effecting The Bargain For Compensation

Many economic and behavioral influences can be proposed to describe the environment in which the employee-employer bargain takes place. Some of the more important influences shown at the bottom of Figure I are described below:

1.   Unemployment Compensation

The Social Security Act of 1935 established the principle that the American worker should be protected by society from total economic destitution in the event he becomes unemployed through no fault of his own. The term "no fault of his own" implies that the worker becomes unemployed because the company has no further "need" for his services for an indefinite period of time. Normally, his lay-off would be caused by a down-turn of business activity. The law indirectly, and subtly, establishes a "minimum wage" for all companies which might offer a job to a formerly employed worker. The worker has the option of accepting unemployment compensation benefits in preference to taking a job not considered "suitable" to his normal line of work and pay level. Presumably he would not accept a job providing a lower total income than does his unemployment compensation. Thus the unemployment compensation *is* the minimum wage for that worker.

2.   Minimum Wage

One of the provisions of the Fair Labor Standards Act of 1938 was to establish a minimum legal hourly wage for all employees "engaged in the production of goods for interstate and foreign commerce."[17]   Such workers obviously constitute a substantial sector of the entire national labor force and, therefore, the law *tends* to drive all wages to a higher level than they would be without such a law. Critics of the law contend that it tends, in contributing to the inflational spiral, to accomplish exactly the opposite of its true purpose. The fact remains that the law exercises a clear influence upon the employer-employee bargain for compensation by setting a floor on wages below which most employers cannot legally bargain. In 1938, the minimum wage was established at 25 cents per hour. The law has been successively revised until the minimum wage is now $1.80 per hour, or more, in most parts of the country.[18]

3.   Job Evaluation

Job Evaluation is defined as "The process of determining the relative values of individual jobs in a given organization so as to establish a wage classification system for that organization."[19]   This definition indicates that any job evaluation plan is an instrument for determining the differential in pay between any two jobs within a given company. It is a means, internal to the company, providing face validity to the internal wage and/or salary structure within the company.
Two general approaches are taken to job evaluation in American industry:

a)   Non-quantitative Methods.   The non-quantitative methods provide a framework by which the evaluator endeavors to determine which, of any two jobs, is the more valuable to the company, or requires the greater preparation and skill, and consequently should command the greater compensation. The evaluator presumably makes an overall judgement between every possible pair of jobs within the company and thus develops a rank-order list of value for all jobs within the company. No attempt is normally made to develop a definitive analysis of all the various factors within each job which contribute to its value or lack of value. If the job evaluation plan permits two or more jobs of approximately equal value to be considered, thus placing the two jobs in a discrete "classification," the plan is usually referred to as a "job classification" method of job evaluation. On the other hand, if each job in the company is placed in a discrete rank-order, the technique is often called a "Rank-order" method of job evaluation.

b)   Quantitative Methods.   The quantitative methods involve breaking down each job into a number of factors, each of which is then evaluated. Probably the most common factors employed are: Skill, Effort, Responsibility, and Job Conditions. Under the "Point" system of job evaluation, a master key is set up by which the evaluator is given a range of values from which he may select the appropriate value for each of the various factors being considered for each job. The grand total of all points for a given job establishes its numerical value with reference to all other jobs evaluated in the company.

The "Factor Comparison" method of job evaluation is somewhat similar to the "Point" method, but requires the evaluator to establish his own master key of factor values, based upon already-existing job relations within a company.

A job evaluation plan thus influences the employer-employee bargaining for compensation because, once a company operates on an established, accepted job-evaluation plan, each job in the company is assigned a specific rate range which establishes the maximum and minimum pay which that job can command. Thus the flexibility for employer-employee bargaining is substantially limited. Presumably the company hopes that the potential employee will recognize sufficient face validity in the system that he will accept a job without questioning the range of compensation to which he is assigned. Through job evaluation, the company establishes specific pay scales for specific jobs in the company, thus eliminating the bargaining process when a new employee enters the organization.

4.   The Company Profit Motive

The ultimate increase in company profits can be a result, among other things, of a reduction in production costs. Since compensation is a major cost of production, it is self-evident that an effort to increase profit can tend to reduce the compensation level of employees.   This does not, however, obviate the fact that a progressive company might easily *increase* compensation in the hope of motivating a higher level of production which would result in increased *long-term* profits.

5.   Union Activity

A union, by definition, is a group of employees who collectively attempt to increase the compensation benefits of their members.   It is, therefore, self-evident that union activity tends to raise the compensation level in the company.

6.   "Going Rates of Pay"

Any private American enterprise presumably competes in the labor market with two kinds of competitors: (a) all other employers within the surrounding community or normal commuting area, and (b) all employers in the entire country who seek employees with the same skills or attributes as the company in question.   In category (b), we assume a mobility of population which permits the movement of an employee's household into the commuting area of the employer.

An attempt by any employer to pay exactly the same rate for a given skill, as that paid by his competitor, under either condition (a) or (b) above will tend to stratify pay scales, immobilize poplulation, and freeze compensation levels in very much the same way as does job evaluation.

7.   Technological Displacement of Labor

Technological displacement of labor (replacing human labor with machines), tends to lower compensation levels. Machines, new methods, and new systems are developed to reduce overall costs by replacing the need for human work, and thus eliminating employees. This displacement adds to the rolls of the unemployed. Through the action of supply-and-demand, the displaced employee is presumably willing to accept a lower compensation to become again employed. However, the employer compares the monetary cost of the new machine or method with the cost of the employee's compensation. We can naturally expect the employer to choose the lower of the two alternative costs. Again, this process tends to force compensation downward.

Categories Of Compensation Factors

The literature reveals numerous ways by which compensation authorities have chosen to categorize the various factors of compensation. A few of the more common sets of categories are discussed below, with the purposes of identifying some of the differences between the various approaches, and of justifying the writer's own selection of categories:

The National Industrial Conference Board has chosen the following set of categories:[20]

1. Straight rate or salary
2. Extra pay for time worked
3. Pay for time *not* worked (while employee is not on company property)
4. Payments for employee security provisions
5. Payments for (costs of) employee services

Sargent has given a similar, but distinctly different set of categories:[21]

1. Straight pay rate or salary
2. Pay for time not worked
3. Payments to provide employee security
4. Practices and services that benefit employees
5. Monetary awards and prizes for special activities and performance
6. Bonuses, contributions, and profit sharing

The difference between the above two categorizations is that Sargent has chosen to distinguish, in his categories #5 and #6, between "awards and prizes" and "bonuses, etc." whereas the NICB understandably combines the two categories into "extra pay for time worked."

A third set of categories defined by Fisher and Chapman is:[22]

1. Straight pay rate or salary
2. Premiums for time worked
3. Pay for time *not* worked
4. Employee benefits
5. Employee activities

Fisher and Chapman's categories closely resemble those of the NICB except that they have chosen to label "employee benefits" what others more specifically label "security benefits." The label "employee benefits" seems to imply the inclusions of more factors than pure "security benefits."

Belcher has chosen the following set of categories:[23]

1. Straight rate or salary
2. Extra payments for time worked
3. Payments for time *not* worked
4. Payments for employee security
5. Payments for employee services
6. Non-production awards and bonuses

Belcher's categories are very similar to those of the NICB except that he has added the last category of "Non-production awards and bonuses" which does not even appear in the NICB group.

All of the above four sets of categories address themselves to the question, "What employee condition, behavior, or need existed which originally caused this factor to be paid by the company?"

Zollitsch and Langsner have suggested quite a different approach to these categories:[24]

1. Straight pay rate or salary
2. Supplements that directly pay their way
3. Supplements that do not directly pay their way

Here, the question seems to be "How closely do factors of compensation relate to the actual production of an employee?" The third category has been described by Victor Vroom as, "Unconditional rewards; in which the amount of reward that an individual receives is not dependent in any way on how he behaves within the organization, but rather on the sole fact that he *is* a member of the organization."[25]

The U.S. Chamber of Commerce has employed a different set of categories:[26]

1. Straight rate or salary
2. Payments for time *not* worked
3. Pension and other agreed-upon payments (employer's share only)
4. Other items
5. Legally required payments (employer's share only)
6. Paid rest periods, lunch periods, travel time, etc.

In the above set, the question seems to be posed, "What conditions originally established this particular factor of compensation?" Belcher has suggested yet another set of categories:[27]

1. Financial rewards in the form of wages and salaries including incentive payments
2. Indirect financial compensation
3. Non-financial, or psychological, compensation

For the sake of the study described in this paper, the writer has chosen a set of categories similar to Belcher's but with the additional variation that "Indirect financial compensation" is divided into two categories, namely, "Employee ownership delayed or contingent upon some predetermined condition," and "Monetary value received in kind; not in cash." The four final categories, with descriptive examples, are shown in Figure II, and the balance of this paper will be developed on the basis of that set of categories. This set evolved from the question, "For a given factor of compensation, how does the employee's real value received compare to the company's cost in providing that factor?"

The foregoing logically brings us to draw an economic comparison, for every factor of compensation, between the cost to the company and the total real value received by the employee. A clear cost comparison provides the company with a position from which to attempt to maximize the economic value exacted through each factor of compensation as compared to the real compensation value received by the employee. From a business management standpoint, the maximization of value received from each factor of compensation can be considered the ultimate purpose of any compensation program.

Each of the categories of compensation in Figure II carries a different degree of income tax liability to the employee. All factors received under "Direct Financial" compensation bear the full brunt of income tax liability, since the employee actually takes title to a cash value.

In the second category, "Employee Ownership delayed or contingent upon some predetermined condition," income tax liability is deferred until such time as the actual money is received by the employee.

This category includes such factors as "Group Insurance," and "Term Life Plans," through which any value received by the employee is normally contingent upon his remaining in the company until reaching a given age, or a given minimum period of service. Presumably such benefits would accrue to the estate of the employee, upon his death, and according to the normal treatment of life insurance benefits, would not incur inheritance taxes. Also, they would incur lower income taxes than if the same value had been received during the life of the employee.

Conversely, Severance Pay, for example, is contingent upon the predetermined condition that the employee will have left his membership in the organization. So long as the employee remained with the organization, no actual monetary value would be conveyed to him through this factor and, of course, no income taxes would be paid by him for the "promisory" value he received from the company.

In the third category, "Monetary Value Received in Kind," it is suggested that the employee receives value from the company for which he might otherwise be paying his own money. However, since it is received "in kind," the employee would, in most cases, pay no income tax for that value received. But in every instance of this factor, the company is incurring a definite, measurable, irretrievable cost.

In the fourth category, "Non-financial or Psychological" compensation, the company may incur some actual capital cost, such as for office appointments or parking facilities for the employee; however, where such cost does occur, it forever remains a capital asset to the company, and title is not conveyed to the employee. A situation is thereby created in which the company is paying compensation to the employee while *retaining 100% of the value* of that compensation, yet paying no profit taxes for its cost. Apparently both the company and the employee benefit from these Non-financial factors of compensation. Nobody pays taxes on them, the employee receives compensation, yet the company retains title to the factor of compensation.

FIGURE II

A MODEL OF THE FACTORS OF COMPENSATION

DIRECT FINANCIAL	INDIRECT FINANCIAL		NON-FINANCIAL OR PSYCHOLOGICAL
	Employee ownership delayed (1 year or more) or contingent upon some predetermined condition	Monetary value received in _kind_, not in cash	
Employee pays income tax in the same year factor is received.	Income tax delayed or reduced	No income tax paid by employee	No income tax paid by employee
Straight rate or salary	Pensions (retirement)	Health & Accident Insurance (company paid)	Status, Prestige
Bonus (paid in cash)	Funded Plans a. Savings	Company Housing	Title, Position
Profit-Sharing (when paid in cash or value recorded as income that year)	b. Profit-sharing c. S.U.B.	Company Transportation	Geographical location
Incentive Payments	Stock Options	Travel	Office, location and appointments
Pay for time not at work (vacation, holidays, sick pay, Reserve duty, jury duty, public service)	Life Insurance	Education Costs (for employee and/or dependents)	Parking facilities (private & reserved)
	Severence Pay	Dues (country club, professional assoc., service clubs)	Secretarial assistance (particularly when a status symbol)
Inconvenience Pay (shift premiums, overtime, work on holidays & weekends)	Social Security (Company's contribution)	Clothing, cleaning	Freedom to establish one's own:
	Guaranteed Wage or salary	Merchandise discounts	a. working time b. project selection
Stock Payments (where employee takes full title to ownership that year)		Legal Aid	c. work methods
		Financial Advice	Non-accountability
Paid rest periods (time when under company control but not expected to work)		Use of company property	Prizes and awards
		Expense accounts	Authority
		Religious facilities	Company Prestige
		Recreation facilities	Public Acclaim
		Workmen's Compensation	Opportunity to create
		Health Care (company provided facilities and/or services)	Job Security
		Special Personnel Services	Opportunity to "serve society"

NOTES

[1]Charles W. Brennon, *Wage Administration* (Homewood, Illinois: Richard Irwin Company, 1963), p. 16.

[2]David W. Belcher, *Compensation Administration* (Englewood Cliffs: Prentice-Hall, 1974), p. 20.

[3]J. M. Greene, "An Analysis of Scientific Management Wage Theories, *Advanced Management*, November 1959, p. 17.

[4]H. G. Zollitsch and A. Langsner, *Wage & Salary Administration* (Cincinnati: South-Western Publishing Company, 1970), p. 121.

[5]Belcher, op.cit., 1974, p. 20.

[6]Ibid., p. 21.

[7]John Maynard Keynes, *The General Theory of Employment Interest and Money* (New York: Harcourt, Brace & Company, 1936).

[8]Majorie S. Turner, "Wages in the Cambridge Theory of Distribution," *Industrial and Labor Relations Review* (April 1966), pp. 390-401.

[9]Henry Ford, *My Life and Work* (New York: Doubleday, Page & Company, 1924).

[10]H.M. Gitelman, "An Investment Theory of Wages," *Industrial & Labor Relations Review* (April 1968), pp. 323-352.

[11]John T. Dunlop, (ed.)., *Theory of Wage Determination* (New York: St. Martins, 1957).

[12]Richard H. Leftwich, *The Price System and Resource Allocation* (New York: Holt, Rinehart & Winston, 1966).

[13]John B. Clark, *Distribution of Wealth* (New York: MacMillan Company, 1899).

[14]H. G. Heneman and Dale Yoder, *Labor Economics* (Cincinnati: South-Western Publishing Company, 1965) p. 607.

[15]Adam Smith, *An Inquiry into the Nature and Causes of the Wealth of Nations* (Scotland: Adam and Charles Black, 1863).

[16]John Davidson, *The Bargaining Theory of Wages* (New York: Putnam Sons, 1898).

[17]Op. cit., Zollitsch and Langsner, p. 45.

[18]Ibid., p. 46.

[19]Ester Becher, *Dictionary of Personnel and Industrial Relations* (New York: Philosophical Library, Inc. 1958), p. 160.

[20]Charles W. Sargent, *Fringe Benefits: Do We Know Enough About Them?* (Hanover: Amos Tuck School of Business Administration, 1953).

[21]"Computing Cost of Fringe," *Studies in Pers. Pol. #128*, NICB 1952.

[22]Austin M. Fisher and John F. Chapman, "Big Costs of Little Fringes," *Harvard Business Review*, Sept.-Oct. 1954, pp. 35-44.

[23]David Belcher, *Wage & Salary Administration* (Englewood Cliffs: Prentice-Hall, Inc., 2nd ed., 1962), p. 489.

[24]Zollitsch & Langsner, p. 621.

[25]Victor Vroom, "The Role of Compensation In Motivation Employees," *Best's Insurance News*, Vol. 67, No. 12, April 1967, pp. 67-74.

[26]*Employee Benefits*, 1967, p. 9.

[27]Belcher, p. 476.

CHAPTER 4

THE DOUBLE-TRACK COMPENSATION AND PROGRESSION SYSTEM

In chapter three, an attempt was first made to outline and describe some of the predominant historical and classical theories of compensation. In response to one or more of these theories, employer and employee seek to establish the level at which their exchange of values shall take place (compensation, in return for work). Next, a brief view was taken of some of the more pronounced influences, largely man-made, which tend to raise, to lower, or to stratify the compensation paid to a given employee. Thirdly, an investigation was made of the various means, methods, or forms in which compensation is conveyed by the employer to the employee.

In this chapter an investigation will be made of the functions and characteristics of a manager as compared to the functions and characteristics of the "professional individual contributor." The double-track system will be described as an instrument by which the employer may seek to provide optimum inducement to every employee to direct his own career progress up the particular side of the double-track ladder which will optimize the economic benefit to his employer and satisfaction to himself.

The "Management" Track

Fuller's version of the functions of management are:

(1) To determine or make decisions.
(2) To communicate.
(3) To do.
(4) To control.[1]

Before a manager is able to "do" and to "control," he must have the authority. This authority may take the form of any one of three recognized types--line, staff or functional.[2] There exists within a bureaucracy a prescribed limit on individual action in the exercise and discretion of action. There is a set system of rules to govern the manager's actions.[3]

When a manager adapts himself to the restrictions imposed by the policies and procedures of the organization, he may still fall short in his quest for excellence. Two reasons are apparent. First, a successful, efficient manager must become dynamic in the control of those whom he must direct. This is a fundamental principle of leadership essential to the function of control.[4]

Second, good organization is based upon "functions" to be performed. Because this is true, choice of management personnel must forego consideration of personalities. The selection of incumbents for management positions must not be made based upon the need to "reward" one for "services" performed.[5]

According to Lunnberg, there are three functions of an executive. These are described as:[6]

(1) Homeostatic--concern with the management of the organization.
(2) Mediative--concern with the internal change in response to environmental pressure.
(3) Proactive--concern with inducing change in the environment to use internal organizational resources.

In a survey conducted by *Forbes*,[7] top executives across the country were asked to describe how they view their function. Of the six top executives surveyed, all responded that their major function was to "cope with the ways that governmental-induced social changes were affecting their business."

Russell De Young of Goodyear reported that his most important function was "to make footsteps that were followed." For him, it was important to bring his influence to bear; in some small way to produce an awareness of the need of Americans to work rather than to "goof off."[8]

A. W. Clausen of the Bank of America viewed his function to be that of keeping "visible and informed." Although the executive cannot run the business alone, he must be informed and in touch with those who do.[9]

In simplified terms, an executive's function is to inspire, cajole, flatter, teach, and induce others to serve in unison with their best effort to achieve a given goal.[10]

In 1937 when Luther Gulick codified the functions of the executive, he did not include "motivation" as a function, for he was of the era when men still responded to models of behavior provided for them by top management.[11]

As late as 1962 there was still very little reported in the professional literature concerning empirical studies relating the actual motivation process to a function of the executive. Silence on the subject suggests the assumed correlation of motivation, per se, with general executive interaction with his subordinates.[12]

In the year 1962, the second edition of Belcher's *Wage and Salary Administration*[13] did cover the definition of an executive's function. This definition was to serve as a foundation for motivating managers through compensation administration. According to the author, an executive's work is defined as:

(1) Creating production and jobs.
(2) Making decisions.
(3) Providing leadership.
(4) Allocating resources.
(5) Reconciling claimant interests.
(6) Introducing innovations.
(7) Accumulating and using capital.
(8) Taking risks.

Managers perform all of the functions. However, there does exist a variance in the degree of responsibility a manager has for the performance of these functions. The level at which he is placed in the organization's hierarchy will determine the variance.

Characteristics Of A Manager

Some observers believe that, by identifying certain universal functions that are performed by all managers, one establishes those characteristics common to successful executives. Then, by evaluating these characteristics in light of his own, a professional should be able to determine whether or not his mental make-up might be complimentary to the tasks required of him in his role as a manager/executive.

To begin the identification process, one needs to make a critical review of what a survey of top company executives viewed as traits that would take one to the top. In making this survey, *Nation's Business* found that there were both positive and negative traits to be considered in appraising the potential success of an executive.[14]

Positive factors were described as:

(1) Intelligence
(2) Drive
(3) Hard work--belief in the free enterprise system
(4) Leadership

Negative factors were described as:

(1) "Know-it-all" attitude
(2) Lack of patience
(3) Impulsiveness
(4) Lack of integrity

One major positive trait agreed upon by all who were surveyed was "total commitment to one's job." The most negative characteristic was "personal ambition in excess of loyalty to the company."

Today, would-be executives have a need to be fulfilled in their role of manager. Their concern for success is all-encompassing. They are competitive in every stance of their lives.[15]

Typically, the executive demonstrates a need to be "master of his own fate," and sets for himself standards that can be achieved by only a few. Often, his standard is an impossible one against which to measure his success. This is a critical characteristic of the successful executive, for the constant dissatisfaction with the status quo makes him a dynamic individual.[16]

According to the survey of executives conducted by *Forbes*, and cited earlier, the intangible characteristics that are attributed to an executive may be best recognized by the following: Why do men take the "hot seat" as executives when they could earn comfortable livelihoods in positions of less extreme exposure?

> The executive's seat is no easy chair in modern America. . .he may find himself 'tossed out' if anything goes wrong. . .they enjoy being always on the 'firing line.'[17]

Generally, an executive may be described as one who grasps the opportunity to demonstrate his ability. His need for making an impact upon his environment is monumental! He requires power to control not only people, but resources. He views every challenge within the organizational structure as an avenue through which he can realize his potential for self-expression.[18]

One must sacrifice much in his life to fulfill the ultimate pursuit of his quest for excellence as an executive. A logical question arises: What is the price placed upon the achievement of self-esteem or self-actualization, and are there rewards equal to the price to be paid?

Tangible Executive Compensation

What is fair pay for an executive?   From the preceding discussion, it is apparent that, just as companies vary in their value assessment placed upon the contribution of an executive to a company, so does the executive's view vary as to what he believes his contribution is worth to the company.

Malcolm S. Salter in 1972 provided a classical definition of what a compensation policy has come to mean within the industrial complex. The definition is stated as follows:

> A scheme of pay differentials which attempts to scale the value of the individual's contribution, thereby forcing the company. . .and the individual, himself. . .to answer questions about the value of his work.[19]

The initial suggestion within the definition is that there exists a scheme or a structure of differentials.   The author continues to develop an understanding of this "scheme" by separating the varying aggregates of the differentials.   He classifies these as:[20]

(1) Perspective of equity.
(2) Norms of equitable payment.
(3) Risks of inequity.

Perspective of equity:

This first aspect of a compensation differential refers to a technique.   One compares the social and professional strengths that an executive brings to his job with the total satisfaction that he takes away from it.

In Kerr's manpower studies made for the year 2000, he identifies a shift in attitude toward the role an executive is called upon to play. From these predictions, he suggests that the executive of the future must possess unique social awareness to cope with changing social forces.   By its dynamic nature, an industrialized society encourages the active role of the highly competitive executive because the imperative is to conquer the old by the new.[21]

By 1980, according to Kerr, our nation will have completed the process of industrialization.[22] With the close of this era, there will arise new patterns of relationships between the "manager" and the "managed."[23]

From the beginning, the process of industrialization of America included a separate consideration of the replacement of the "old collective" with a "new" one. A movement toward a centralized state gained momentum throughout the past decades. Diverse interests of the populace created an environment in which the plural needs and aspirations of the nation's citizens had to be recognized and dealt with in some workable fashion. Thus, the executive in industry or government today must possess social awareness.[24]

A pluralistic society offers to the aspiring executive alternative routes to success.   Initially, however, many candidates for top management positions do not have the social awareness necessary to conquer the divergent demands made of him by society. Only the socially strong candidate will eventually achieve the elite position that is the reward for his social conquest.[25]

Social awareness is further emphasized when one understands that the middle-class segment of our American society provides the majority of top-level executives. Thus, the struggle to achieve success is a traumatic one for those candidates who are products of the second-level echelon of our stratified society.

The elite of our stratified society have accrued to themselves places in this elevated strata by virtue of "power by position." The "old elites" are of the minority today in our nation. However, these static minorities still dominate the power structure in industry. Position is maintained from one generation to another through the transfer of the power base as well as superior educational opportunities. Ultimately, the elite rise to positions of "chairman of the board," and avail themselves to the services of a capable person as their Chief Executive Officer, which perpetuates the process.[26] It is therefore inferred that compensation is geared, in large measure, to the social awareness the executive brings to his position.

A correlation of compensation and an executive's managerial strength must incorporate the requirement that a successful executive be a trained critical thinker. The most valuable executive will be one who has developed an ability intuitively to hypothesize relationships. He will be one who arrives at a correct decision in making order of old knowledge in modern concepts of application.[27]

Both the organization and the individual must be satisfied with the compensation package offered and accepted.   The executive's satisfaction will generally be defined differently at each successive step up the career ladder.

For the "junior" executive, the amount of salary received is vitally important if he is to be "satisfied" with his particular position. However, as an executive succeeds and is elevated to the extent that he can afford the outward manifestations of status, salary alone, in the compensation package, does not provide for him the satisfaction he requires.

The top executive's satisfaction is derived largely from intangible benefits in the compensation scheme. For example, from a 1970 survey it was found that a large portion of a top executive's satisfaction was derived from his association with a peer group of equal drive.[28]

Norms of equitable payment:

This second consideration of compensation differentials is important. Within this element an attempt is made to match compensation for levels of decision-making authority to an executive's ideas of what is "fair" compensation for the decisions he must make.

An executive's functions include the planning process. This function is performed at every level of management, however, the degree to which the import of an executive's planning is felt upon the organization is contingent upon his placement within the hierarchy. Decision-making is a critical aspect of the planning process. It is required of all managers, and the importance of the decision is measured in terms of its consequences.[29]

Decision-making is defined as:

the selection of one behavior alternative from two or more possible alternatives. . .to divide means. . .to come to a conclusion.[30]

The extent to which an executive's decision-making results in the altering of a course of action for a given magnitude is also an index of the "fair" price to be paid for this aspect of his managerial function.

Risks of inequity:

Responsibility and exposure increase concurrently for the executive. Thus, a company must create within its compensation package a clear-cut differentiation between these packages at the defined managerial levels. To compensate an individual for accepting the "risks" of failure, a gap is deliberately created between middle managers and executives.[31] One of the more effective current methods used to create this required gap is the "cafeteria plan."[32]

In choosing his particular "package," the executive will be influenced by many factors, some of which directly relate to his relative position within the organization. For example, because an executive must be not only a creative leader but a skillful delegator of responsibility, he must be prepared to accept high risks associated with his actions. A portion of his compensation package will be a deferred payment plan or arrangement whereby he is guaranteed a salary base that will permit him to maintain some of the status symbols he prizes even when a younger man replaces him.[33] The deferred payment plan serves to insulate the executive against the risks associated with his change in company affiliation.[34]

Members of a dynastic elite were originally drawn from the aristocracy of our nation. These members formed a "closed shop," and created a social strata. The executive's primary goal is often his aspiration to reach the elite's strata. To achieve his aspiration, the executive's salary must be sufficient to enable him to maintain a life style consistent with the elite strata.[35] Once he attains a life stye consistent with the image of his top-level management position, he may then concentrate on other selections for his compensation package.[36]

The "Professional" Track

Part of the "rewards" of a professional are that he is recognized by his professional peers. The satisfaction in his work situation is enhanced by his reasonably compatible level of pay compensation coupled with his "freedom" to choose his goals, and approaches to their attainment. But when the professional becomes a manager, he may be plagued with a sense of frustration caused by his lack of control of the functions of his operation. The trained manager understands that the command of his position may often be diluted because he is an integral part of an organization. The manager is trained to respond to efforts to accommodate organizational demands and individual needs. This may be a basic difference between the professional-turned-manager and the trained manager.[37]

Status, prestige, and power can often persuade a professional to change tracks, and become a manager. What accounts for this apparently illogical move? Generally, the need to achieve--the need for self-actualization causes the stable, successful professional to "cross over."[38]

All too frequently there is little consideration given, at any level of an organization, to the potential career development of the professional outside his field of expertise. Yet, once a professional has proven himself within his own field, and has through such means as research publications, "made a name" for himself, it follows that this individual is often considered for management positions. He has proven himself to be a successful individual contributor, and for that very reason has been chosen, somewhat illogically, to manage people.

Up to a certain point, in government or industry, an individual's career will be measured largely by his increasing competency in his field of specialty. Recognition will be accorded to an individual by his colleagues in their searching him out for guidance in their own undertakings. The organization will reward him through increased salary compensation and promotions to "titled" positions. However, for the successful person in the scientific or specialized disciplines, there may come a time when there are no additional promotions available within his "track." He must "cross over" to a position of managerial responsibility if he is to continue to "grow" in his quest for self-actualization.[39]

Initial Reaction To Change Of Tracks

The initial reaction of a professional to a proposed radical shift is usually one of concern. Heretofore, his value to the company has been gauged by what he, personally, could accomplish using his technical know-how. However, the criterion of his value as a manager must necessarily be that of how successful he will be in getting others to do things.[40]

Moreover, the practice of his professional expertise is an inherent and vital part of his life. He has come to believe in a lasting commitment to his work. To the highly dedicated professional, there appears to be some contradiction in the options that are open to him. Surely, he too, seeks recognition and esteem like the manager. However, the question must arise as to the value of his technical "brain power" as a source of energy for the continued industrial growth of his company. Because of his acknowledgement of the need to keep abreast of rapidly changing technology, he has had little time consciously to concern himself with preparation for a managerial role.

Thus, after a scientist, for example, is confronted with the initial proposal to make the transition from scientist to manager, he may ultimately reason in one of two manners.

First, the fundamentalist will consider the duties and responsibilities entailed in the managerial position for which he is considered. He will analyze the personal implications for him. That is, will there be adequate retraining to permit his becoming a successful manager? Can he divorce himself from his role as a technical specialist and ignore the tremendous investment in his professional training for his current profession? Finally, is the recognition and esteem worth the price?[41]

The second type will be one who is eternally optimistic about his chance of success, and will have few reservations concerning his succeeding in the proposed new undertaking. His attitude toward "management" may be such that he does not generally accord it the classification of a "science." From his vantage point, anyone of average intelligence should be able to "master" the practice of management.[42]

This second individual will probably weigh only one factor in the balance: What esteem will accrue as a result of the transition?

Why The Cross-Over?

At this point, it is appropriate to investigate: (1) why professionals cross-over from the "professional" track to the "manager" track, (2) whether or not the desire for power and prestige is equally operative in those who cross-over as compared with those who do not cross-over.

Myers' 1961 study of the Texas Instruments Company tested Herzberg's theory of motivation.[43] The study was designed to determine whether there was still a valid correlation between Herzberg's test at Western Reserve University on scientists and accountants. Myers found that scientists were those who are most strongly motivated by quest for achievement. Pay was important to scientists (engineers especially) only to the extent that it derived its importance primarily from status factors.[44]

This finding correlated with that of David C. McClelland who described the "Motive A" personality, and who ascribed such a personality to many research scientists. According to McClelland, a research scientist who possesses a "Motive A" personality cannot devote his life to an endeavor with slow feedback time. He requires ego food that is not forthcoming from his scientific endeavors after a particular period in his career.[45]

Promotions (with corresponding pay increases) will serve to satisfy the need to be recognized up to a certain point in an aggressive scientist's career. However, as he strives for self-actualization and the higher order needs of esteem and recognition, this "reward" becomes an inadequate one.[46] This is especially true of the scientist who is a governmental employee because it is he who notes the limitations placed upon his salary by Congressional Acts. It is he who learns the double standard of recognition. For, like most government scientists, he is afforded an opportunity clearly to understand the power structure. He recognizes at what level prestige is accorded. Irrespective of the number of important contributions he may have to "science," deference is shown to the GS-15 Associate Deputy. That is, when the two equally ranked general schedule employees appear together to perform a function within the scope of a group of fellow employees, deference is shown to the "manager."

In such a situation repeated many times over, pay and a high numerical ranking do not serve the scientist as positive reinforcement for the recognition of his professional accomplishments. Rather, the scientist notes that his fellow scientist who "gave up" his productive research career to become a sometimes-frustrated manager, is also the person to whom esteem is accorded. At this juncture, the successful research scientist begins to aspire to become a member of the top echelon of the "power elite." Aspirations are often dynamic forces for illogical change.

The professional is not one who has suddenly become a competitive person, seeking rewards and self-fulfillment. On the contrary, he has usually devoted years to his professional pursuit. However, the lure of the other side of the dual track system often creates a less self-centered attitude towards his dedication to his all-consuming research. He begins to ponder the position in which he will find himself for the remainder of his life. He may tend to become unsure of his personal identity, and to question the value of his research in the future. Then, time becomes a factor! He, by the fortunes of fate, is provided with a "rare" chance to do something even more important! The successful scientist turns from his career to become a "top manager." At last, he, too, will prove his versatility. He will have an opportunity to exercise control over human beings, as well as goods and materials.[47]

To illustrate the causes and effects of the "cross-over," the following actual case is given involving a federal government employee. By reference to the principle of "the universality of management" the reader will recognize that the characteristics and environment in this government agency would be virtually identical to those in private industry.

A Case Example: U.S. Dept. Of Agriculture [48]
Cross-Over From Scientist To Manager

The Agricultural Research Service historically has replenished its rank of top administrators from the professional side of the dual track. The idea has prevailed within ARS that top executives, recruited from the scientific track, could be utilized as understudies and thus "learn by doing and imitating." Today, however, whether in industry or within the Agricultural Research Service, management development is a highly sophisticated endeavor. It is one which involves changing a particular individual in ways that alter his competence as a manager. Part of such an endeavor requires the realignment of the candidate's indentity. In ARS, for example, it would entail the careful modification of the manager's concern with the "set aside" of his professional identity.[49]

In a segment of *Management in the Modern Organization,*[50] an apt description is provided of the obstacle course to be run by the ARS scientist turned manager. The authors have specified the role of manager by suggesting that the "chief executive" in business or government "expands his activities and increases his horizon." In this, the case of the ARS Deputy Administrator for the Southern Region, the first move was to recruit this outstanding Agricultural Engineer from his field-level position where he had been barely exposed to any *significant* decision-making. By the power and prestige "carrot" he was lured to the Washington hierarchy to "understudy" the executive functions of the Agricultural Research Service.

In his research endeavor, there had been fewer and fewer new opportunities to "grow" within the organization. Thus, by crossing over to the "manager" track, he could become a meaningful figure in shaping a new organizational structure. It was an "ego boost" to be "called-out;" to be allowed to use his aggressive nature to become an inventive; to be given the organizational latitude to mold policy and shape lives.

Yet, as he contemplated his decision to cross-over from the scientific track to the administrative one, he was filled with doubts and questions. He perceived the shortcomings that he might carry with him to the new administrative position. Specifically, he was concerned about the academic aspect of a line and staff relationship. The scientist realized his inability to transfer his expertise in the field of agricultural engineering to that of a top manager. Certainly, he would find his previous experience as a scientist to his benefit in recognizing valuable research goals brought to his attention. However, a fundamental and basic question should have been posed much earlier. "Should a top manager in the Agricultural Research Service be picked because of his technical knowledge and experience in the Service? Or, should such a manager be picked because of his demonstrated application of managerial skills learned in an academic endeavor?"

Fuller says, concerning the question of technical competence versus management skills:

> Promotion to management does not automatically make you a manager. The placing of a laurel wreath of authority on one's brow has no such magical effect. Management skill is NOT a by-product of promotion.[51]

If a top manager is to perform his executive function, he cannot continue to operate as a technical specialist; not a technical specialist aligned, for example, with the science of engineering. Rather, the effective manager must be content with his important task of planning, organizing, coordinating, and leading. He must relinquish his place as a technical specialist. To a subordinate he must look for information required on given subject-matter specialties.

Technical qualifications are not enough when the scientist has become a manager. The scientist-turned-manager must learn the "practice" of management, to use the authority, and accept the responsibility for organizing and directing of the work of others.

As the Deputy Administrator in this example assumed his position in Washington, steps were already being taken to dissolve the organizational structure into which he had been placed. Within months, he was transferred to the position of top administrator of the Southern Region. His period as an "understudy" was nil. Instead, he was required to stretch himself far beyond his most expansive view of self-competence within the management area. He was faced with an overwhelming expansion of responsibility for the multi-level disciplines that encompassed all of the Agricultural Research Service. He might have been indoctrinated to his position as "management trainee" concerned with missions and program personnel. Instead, however, this newly recruited administrator suddenly became responsible for many diverse programs with equally diverse personnel.

His basic mission was to establish, in New Orleans, a new system of management of the Southern Regional activities of the Agricultural Research Service. In his expanded role of "Coordinating Officer," there were none around him trained to accept a delegation of authority to carry out any one of the numerous sub-entities of the reorganization. He was surrounded with personal assistants recruited from the scientific track with a firm foundation in their technical specialties but with minimal qualifications for the professional tasks associated with top management.

What is the price of having achieved a top management position? Charles C. Gibbons has suggested that in industry or government, an executive must pay the price, first of all, of being a loner. He must use all of his energy and resources for the maintenance of his dynamic role. He must submit himself to extreme stress that taxes him both psychologically and physiologically.[52]

Stress of the utmost degree was placed upon the ARS manager who was formerly a successful scientist in full command of his research situation. A high magnitude of frustration built up within the "new" manager. The frustration amplified the psychological and physiological nature of the stress impact, for there was a conclusion to be drawn. The scientist, who but a short time ago gave up a productive career as a contributing member of his professional group, discovers the merits of these pronouncements:[53]

> He is not able to coordinate the information available to him, and he cannot plan properly. He finds that he has so many people having

impact upon the decision-making process that he has become, in reality, little more than a nonfunctioning figure head.

He had two alternatives open to him:

(1)   He could face his dilemma, and reverse the loss to his agency of his scientific contribution. He could return to his professional duties where he was competent above others; he could mend his pride by resolving again to produce as a scientist, at an even higher caliber of effort than before.

(2)   Or, he could face the fact that he possessed limited competence in the role of a top manager without benefit of formal training and understudy.   However, he could put aside this truth-encounter and remain in his management position.   In this second situation, he may spend the remainder of his governmental career on the downward slide from his former base of high esteem as a professional to one of relative impotence as a manager.

Epilogue:

The tragic result in the specific case described, is that the first alternative was denied the incumbent.   He had only a choice of the second alternative or "early retirement."   Consequently, this brilliant scientist is still in Washington, D.C., today, heroically trying to fill the managerial position for which he was never prepared, and in which he is generally ineffective, even by his own admission.

One of the few differences between this example within a government agency, and a similar situation in private enterprise, is that this man has the "protection" of the Civil Service System, whereas in industry he could, and probably would be separated from the firm. This leaves us pondering whether the "protection" is truly to his benefit.

Alternatives To The Cross-Over

It may be reasonable to suggest two alternatives to the present shortcoming of many organizations in making promotions from the professional track to that of the managerial one.

Alternative Number One:

First, is the alternative related to the sociology of knowledge.[54] As has been noted earlier, people play the roles dictated by society as being appropriate for status achievers.   Thus, the problem described wherein managers are generally promoted as a "reward" must be eliminated.   This would entail the undertaking of a program to re-educate all employees concerning business management as a profession. By the year 2000, educational requirements for the manager will be dynamic.[55]   These will necessarily be in keeping with theoretical assumptions predicting future technological changes.   Some twenty-odd years from now, it is realistic to expect research to have progressed to a point at which it will far exceed one's grasp of the functional or operational use made of it.   The sociological implications of this are apparent.   Key figures in government and business cannot afford the luxury of obsolescence of attitude.   Management will necessarily be regarded as an art or science in its own right.[56]

The first alternative may well be described as a reorientation of line and staff people to understand the dual track, especially as one relates primordial educational preparation for each.   This education could serve to neutralize the current aspiration by scientists to cross-over, since the intellectually ambitious individual can be taught to understand the futility of two major educational endeavors within his short career span.

Moreover, if the scientist were encouraged to think of his position in relationship to the inverted pyramid, he could be conditioned to value his special technical role in the staffing pattern.   This, coupled with the knowledge that managers must be highly trained in a specific combination of specialties, should permit more self-actualization to occur within the scientist as a result of his constant attention to his specialty. Too, he would necessarily be involved in the process of technical re-education as a life-long process because of the explosion of knowledge of this age and the ever-increasing scientific knowledge expected even 20 years from now.[57]

Alternative Number Two:

If the first proposal of an alternative to the current practice of recruiting top managers from the scientific track is not acceptable to an organization, then the only remaining logical alternative appears to be the acceptance of the practice as "status quo."   In this situation, a major attempt should be made to alter the outlook and objectives of both the professional and the potential manager to the extent that he will not serve his period of time caught up in a web of indecision.   If successful, such an undertaking could eliminate a constant series of "uneducated" reactions to managerial problems that could result in managerial blunders.

The IBM Corp. provides an example of this alternative: Before 1952, IBM began to take their technical personnel and re-train them as professional managers.[58] In this way, the cumbersome transition of the manager in his cross-over from scientific to managerial responsibilities was largely alleviated.

There is abundant evidence in the literature to suggest that in the future a more educated society will demand increasingly more effective, efficient management of its organizations--management which is responsive to dynamic changes in their cultural as well as in their political environment.

Such a demand by society will automatically dictate either that effective managers be recruited for their specific roles or that they be educated on the job, through systematic attention to the process. The rapid changes occurring now within government and society will demand that we discontinue the practice of calling upon professional personnel to fill management positions.[59]

NOTES

[1]Don Fuller, *Manage or Be Managed!* (Boston, Massachusetts: Fransworth Publishing Company, Inc., 1964), pp. 3-18.

[2]Herbert J. Chruden and Arthur W. Shermon, Jr., *Personnel Management* (4th ed.) (Cincinnati, Ohio: South-Western Publishing Company, 1972), pp. 69-71.

[3]James G. March (ed.) *Handbook of Organizations,* "Public Bureaucracies" by Robert L. Peabody and Francis E. Rourke (Chicago, Illinois: Rand McNally and Company, 1965), p. 805.

[4]John F. Mee (ed.) *Personnel Handbook* (New York: The Ronald Press Company, 1951), p. 732.

[5]Ibid., p. 732.

[6]Craig C. Lunnberg, "Planning the Executive Development Program," *California Management Review,* XV (Fall 1972), p. 13.

[7]____, "Buck Stops Here! The Role of the Chief Executive Officer," *Forbes,* 107 (May 1971), p. 47.

[8]Ibid., p. 51.

[9]Ibid., p. 53.

[10]George R. Terry, *Principles of Management* (Homewood, Illinois: Richard B. Irwin, Inc., 1961), p. 87.

[11]James G. March (ed.), *Handbook of Organizations,* p. 389.

[12]David W. Belcher, *Wage and Salary Administration* (2nd ed.) (Englewood Cliffs, N.J.: Prentice-Hall, Inc., 1962), p. 519.

[13]Ibid.

[14]____, "Traits that will take you to the Top," *Nation's Business, 60 (September 1972),* pp. *70-71.*

[15]Theo Haimann and William G. Scott, *Management in the Modern Organization,* p. 7.

[16]F. Bartolome, "Executives as Human Beings", *Harvard Business Review,* 60 (November 1972), p. 28.

[17]____, "Buck Stops Here! The Role of the Chief Executive Officer," *Forbes,* p. 47.

[18]Theo Haimann and William G. Scott, *Management in the Modern Organization, pp. 384-385.*

[19]Malcolm S. Salter, "What is 'Fair Pay' for the Executive?" *Harvard Business Review*, 50 (May 1972), p. 6.

[20]Ibid., pp. 144-146.

[21]Clark Kerr, et al., *Industrialism and Industrial Man* (Cambridge, Massachusetts: Harvard University Press, 1960), p. 47.

[22]Ibid., p. 266.

[23]Ibid., p. 265.

[24]Ibid., pp. 58-65.

[25]Ibid., pp. 1-49.

[26]Ibid.

[27]Richard N. Farmer, *Management in the Future* (Belmont, CA: Wadsworth Publishing Company, Inc., 1967), pp. 18-29.

[28]Jeremy Bacon, "Executive Compensation Plans in the Smaller Company," Report No. 15 *Managing the Moderate-sized Company*, p. 18.

[29]Herbert J. Chruden and Arthur W. Sherman, Jr., *Personnel Management* (4th ed.), p. 94.

[30]George R. Terry, *Principles of Management* (4th ed.), p. 43.

[31]Saul Gellerman, *Behavioral Concepts in Management* (2nd ed.) (Encino, California: Dickinson Publishing Company, Inc., 1972), p. 97.

[32]Jeremy Bacon, "Executive Compensation Plans in the Smaller Company," Report No. 15 *Managing the Moderate-sized Company*, pp. 6-18.

[33]Frank B. Hartman, "Why Executives Need Psychiatrists," *Duns*, 102 (November 1973), pp. 13-17.

[34]Franklin G. Moore (ed.) *A Management Source Book* (New York: Harper & Row Publishers, 1964), pp. 458-465.

[35]Clark Kerr, et al., *Industrialism and Industrial Man*, p. 52.

[36]Ibid., p. 49.

[37]David W. Belcher, *Wage and Salary Administration*, pp. 517-565.

[38]Franklin G. Moore (ed.) *A Management Source Book*, pp. 3-6.

[39]Don Fuller, *Manage or Be Managed!* pp. 1-1.

[40]David R. Hampton, *Modern Management: Issues and Ideas* (Belmont, California: Dickinson Publishing Company, Inc., 1969), p. 300.

[41]Ibid.

42Don Fuller, *Manage or Be Managed!* pp. 1-5.

[43]Scott Myers, "Why Are Your Motivated Workers?" in David R. Hampton's *Behavioral Concepts in Management* (2nd ed.) (Encino, California: Dickinson Publishing Company, Inc., 1972), p. 46.

44
Ibid., p. 57.

[45]David C. McClelland, "The Urge to Achieve," in David R. Hampton's *Behavioral Concepts in Management, pp. 78-81.*

[46]Edward E. Lawler, III. "Motivation and Merit: Pay and Promotion" in David R. Hampton's *Behavioral Concepts in Management,* p. 112.

[47]Harry Levinson, "On Being a Middle-aged Manager," *Harvard Business Review* (July-August 1969), pp. 51-60.

[48]J. W. Crim and B. J. McMurtry, Unpublished survey of U.S. Dept. of Agriculture, Agricultural Research Service, Auburn, Ala.

[49]Craig C. Lunnberg, "Planning the Executive Development Program," *California Management Review,* pp. 10-11.

[50]Theo Haimann and William G. Scott, *Management in Modern Organization,* pp. 200-401.

[51]Don Fuller, *Manage or Be Managed!* pp. 1-2.

[52]Charles C. Gibbons, "Are You Willing to Pay Price for Becoming an Executive?" in Franklin G. Moore (ed.) *A Management Source Book* (New York: Harper & Row Publishers, 1964), pp. 32-45.

[53]Theo Haimann and William G. Scott, *Management in Modern Organization,* p. 211.

[54]Peter L. Berger, *Invitation to Sociology: A Humanistic Perspective,* pp. 110-111.

[55]Richard N. Farmer, *Management in the Future,* pp. 22-23.

[56]Ibid., p. 19.

[57]Ibid., p. 18.

[58]Ibid., pp. 18-19.

59
Ibid., pp. 23-69.

CHAPTER 5

THE SURVEY

As described in "Methodology," the survey was mailed to 250 selected recipients by the American Compensation Association on March 19, 1975. The letter of transmittal was written by Arthur D. Ring, Executive Director of the Association and the mailing accomplished by that office.

By May 17, sixty-three (25.2%) responses had been received, and a second follow-up letter (letter #2) was sent to those who had not responded. Subsequently, thirty-seven (14.8%) additional responses were received, making a total of exactly 100 useable responses (40%) from which conclusions in Chapter 6 were drawn. It should be noted that sixteen letters were received in which respondents explained that, for various reasons, they were unable to participate in our survey. The total gross response to the survey was therefore 46.4%.

Meantime, a special letter (letter #3) was mailed to every person mentioned in question #8 by any of the 100 respondents (". . . considered an authority on the subject of compensating managers and professionals"). An interesting observation regarding the mention of "authorities" in question #8 was: Of those who indicated that their company does have a double-track system, only 35% mentioned any "authority." However, of those that indicated that their company does *not* have a double-track system, 61% gave the name of at least one "authority." Each of forty respondents gave one name as an authority, while nine gave two or more names. One experienced compensation practitioner gave the names of eight authorities. Fifty-one percent of all respondents made no mention of any "authorities'" names whatever.

Question #9 requested that respondents give names of companies which they knew to have had experience in the application or a formal framework of comparative compensation of managers vs. professionals. In most cases, where company names were given, those companies had already been included in the mailings of this survey. In the four cases in which the mentioned company had not already received a questionnaire, and where the company fitted the survey frame of "American Industrial Firm," that company was immediately surveyed. The vast majority of respondents did not list any company in this regard.

In analyzing returned questionnaires, it becomes apparent that question #4 was not eliciting responses which were sufficiently specific (Does your company policy clearly distinguish at least two separate compensation and progression ladders for managers and professionals?). Some respondents answered "No" to the question while adding a scientific and systems department." The implication seemed clear, in such cases, that the respondent interpreted the question as calling for an affirmative answer *only* if the double-track system were company-wide; covering all departments. Other respondents answered "Yes" to the question while adding a comment such as "for technical and sales professionals only." To correct this ambiguity of these responses, another follow-up letter (letter #4) was sent to every respondent who answered "Yes" to question #4. This letter simply listed typical departments in an industrial firm, asking the respondent to check-off those departments in which his company operates a double-track system.

Throughout analysis of the survey data, numerous telephone calls were made to respondents whenever responses required clarification or enlargement. Telephone interviews were held particularly with compensation practitioners established as "authorities" by their peers. This was done when establishing factors which ought to be considered in differentiating the "manager ladder" from that of the "professional."

AUBURN UNIVERSITY

AUBURN   ALABAMA

36830

SCHOOL OF BUSINESS

Department of Management

Telephone 826-4071
Area Code 205

LETTER #2

About two months ago, the American Compensation Association mailed, to a selected list of about 10% of their members, a questionnaire entitled "Survey of Compensation and Progression Ladders for Managers and Professionals". The mailing list included only compensation practitioners associated with industrial firms in the "Fortune 500". To avoid needless duplication, only one person in each firm was contacted. You were the only person in your firm to receive the questionnaire.

We are probing the question, "How do companies administer the compensation and progression of the non-supervisory trained "professional", as compared to that of the "manager" of people ?" We are also seeking to determine the degree to which U.S. industrial firms now have "Double-Track", or "dual" compensation and progression ladders for managers and professionals.

We feel this is an important area of concern in the field of compensation and we hope you will be interested in the ultimate report of our survey, a copy of which we shall send to each respondent.

Since we have not received your reply, we are taking the liberty of enclosing another copy of the questionnaire in the hope you will find it possible to give us the benefit of input from your company. Needless to say, the data will be treated in confidence and no names of persons or companies will be used without specific permission.

Thank you sincerely, for your help.

Yours very truly,

John W. Crim
Asst. Prof. of Management

A LAND-GRANT UNIVERSITY

AUBURN UNIVERSITY

AUBURN · ALABAMA

36830

SCHOOL OF BUSINESS

Department of Management

Telephone 826-4071
Area Code 205

LETTER #3

    I am writing to you because a number of professional compensation people have identified you as an authority in their field.

    About a month ago, the American Compensation Association mailed, to a selected list of about 10% of their members, a questionnaire entitled "Survey of Compensation and Progression Ladders for Managers and Professionals". The mailing list included only compensation practitioners associated with industrial firms in the "Fortune 500". To avoid needless duplication, only one person in each firm was contacted.

    A copy of the questionnaire is enclosed for your reference. You will note that question #8 asks: "Based upon you personal experience, please give the name of any person, anywhere in America, whom you consider to be an authority on the subject of compensating managers and professionals:" We have now received a response to the questionnaire which is numerically satisfactory.

    Your name is among the handful of those given in answer to the above question. Because of this fact, as established by your peers, we would like to ask if you would be kind enough to give us the benefit of your input to our research. This project is being directed by Drs Young, Mescon, Crane, and Henderson of the faculty of the Graduate School of Business, Georgia State University. The results will comprise a major portion of my doctoral dissertation.

    We are probing the question, "How should a company best administer a compensation package for the non-supervisory trained "professional", as compared to that of the "manager" of people?" We are interested in:
    a) What factors <u>ought</u> to be considered in establishing the compensation and status of a "professional", and why?
    b) What factors ought to be used with respect to a "manager", and why?
    c) Should the same formula apply to both the "professional" and the "manager", and why?

    Through the vehicle of the questionnaire, we are seeking to determine the degree to which U.S. industrial firms <u>now</u> have "Double-Track", or separate compensation and progression ladders for managers

LETTER #3 (continued)

and professionals. We hope to find:

a) parameters establishing what type and size of firm may now be distinguishing between the two ladders,

b) how high the professional may conceivably go in his firm, as compared with the manager, and

c) whether firms not now having a dual system may anticipate adopting one in the foreseeable future.

Your personal views on these questions would be most appreciated. Needless to say, they will be treated in confidence and you will be quoted only with your specific permission. We will send you a copy of our final report in the hope that you will find it interesting.

We hope we may look forward to your response.

Yours very truly,

John W. Crim

John W. Crim,
Asst. Prof. of Management

THE SURVEY

AUBURN UNIVERSITY

AUBURN   ALABAMA

36830

SCHOOL OF BUSINESS

Department of Management

Telephone 826-4071
Area Code 205

LETTER #4

You recently were kind enough to complete and return our questionnaire which was mailed to you by the American Compensation Association. It was entitled: "Survey of Compensation and Progression Ladders for Managers and Professionals". We are now evolving some very interesting data, and wish to thank you for your contribution.

You may recall that you answered "Yes" to the question: "Does your company policy clearly distinguish at least two separate compensation and progression ladders for managers and professionals?" For those of you who answered in the affirmative, we would like to ask for one more piece of information which should not take more than a moment of your time:

At the bottom of this letter, would you please indicate in which organizational functions, or departments, you do have a double-track ladder now in operation? Just check the appropriate spaces (or add departments not listed) and return this letter to me at the above address.

Engineering_____	E.D.P./Systems_____
Research_____	Industrial Relations_____
Accounting_____	Mf'g/Industrial Eng'g._____
Finance_____	Prod./Inventory Control____
Marketing_____	Purchasing_____
Legal_____	Other?_____

Thank you, again, for your cooperation. I look forward to sending you the results of this research.

John W. Crim,
Asst. Prof. of Management

A   LAND-GRANT   UNIVERSITY

CHAPTER 6

DESIGN OF EXISTING DOUBLE-TRACK SYSTEMS

In this chapter, several currently-operating double-track systems will be described. This will provide the conceptual framework from which conclusions from the survey will be drawn in Chapter 7.

Figure III depicts a typical double-track system of compensation and progression as defined within a given department of an organization. The configuration is that of the Industrial Research Institute (I.R.I.). The I.R.I. is a national professional association founded in 1938 under the auspices of the National Research Council. Its purpose is to improve the general well-being of scientific research in this country through the exchange of non-proprietary ideas, information, and administrative techniques. Its membership consists largely of scientists in the managerial tracks of their firms.

Titles in Figure III apply to a typical research department of a company. In actual practice this particular configuration is used as a vehicle for the reporting of salary levels employed by member companies for the I.R.I. annual salary surveys. It will be seen that the double-track is divided between the administrative (A group) on the left, and the technical (T group) on the right. The assumption is that the recent graduate engineer or physicist enters the organization at position number 1 at the bottom of the diagram. Presumably his position represents his relationship to the rest of the organization both in salary, and status and prestige. Normally, the incumbent progresses to position number 2. At his next promotion he approaches the decision upon which the entire double-track system is founded; whether to pursue the non-supervisory technical track on the right or the management track on the left. Supposedly, position 3-A and 3-T are essentially equal in compensation range and in status. Likewise position 4-A and 4-T are generally equal and 5-A and 5-T are generally equal. However, it is pointed out by the spokesman and Executive Director of the Industrial Research Institute, that "At all levels and for all degrees, the A group has a higher salary for similar year of experience. Also, it appears that the administrative personnel outnumber the technical employees by more than two to one at the highest position level (position number 5-A or 5-T). At the lowest position level at which the double-track method usually begins (level number 3), the ratio is about three to one in the other direction, with technical outnumbering the administrative."

FIGURE III

INDUSTRIAL RESEARCH INSTITUTE

LADDERS

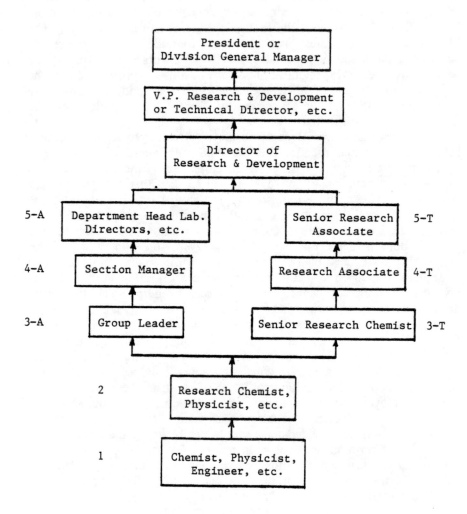

A comparison of the above double-track configuration with specific double-track systems exercised in American industrial firms today will show some interesting differences:

Standard Oil Co. of Ohio, (SOHIO) expands the number of levels throughout the entire system, totalling six position levels below the branch, in the research and development organization, with 20 separate levels or grades above the branch. A significant observation on the plan is that the highest title on the technical side is "Senior Scientist" which presumably is at a compensation and career progress level second only to the overall Manager of Research and Development. Thus the technical progress ladder is "stretched out" considerably more than the three positions shown on the I.R.I. configuration. SOHIO also maintains a separate double-track system for engineering as opposed to research and development. The engineering track is 18 levels above the branching point for the managerial side. SOHIO also uses an informal double-track system in their systems and data processing department.

Standard Oil Company of California, one of the pioneers in the double-track system, maintains a double-track system throughout virtually all departments in the company. Standard of California has an interesting variation as shown in Figure IV. In their arrangement they have three tracks below the branching point, namely, engineer, analyst, and foreman. This provides the incumbent with considerably more than a single dichotomous choice at the branching point. Probably the graduate engineer chooses between the tracks of: (a) pure professional (specialist), (b) supervision of professionals, (c) the analyst track (also an individual contributor type of professional track), or lastly, (d) the conventional line supervisory track. The incumbent, below the branching point, not a graduate engineer or scientist, would presumably be in either the analyst or foreman track and would have the dichotomous choice of proceeding up either the analyst or the line supervisory track. At every level, as the diagram indicates, the compensation and prestige level extends horizontally across all four tracks.

Another interesting variation is employed by the Pittsburgh Plate Glass Company, (PPG), as described by Robert K. Rollf, of PPG Industries, in an address to the National Society of Research Administrators in Houston, Texas, on March 5, 1968. As shown in Figure V, the PPG Company describes three paths above the branching point by which a distinction is made, on the professional side, between the research scientist and the staff engineer. Rollf describes seven problem areas which were pertinent to the implementation and success of their multiple paths of progression program:

FIGURE IV

STANDARD OIL COMPANY OF CALIFORNIA

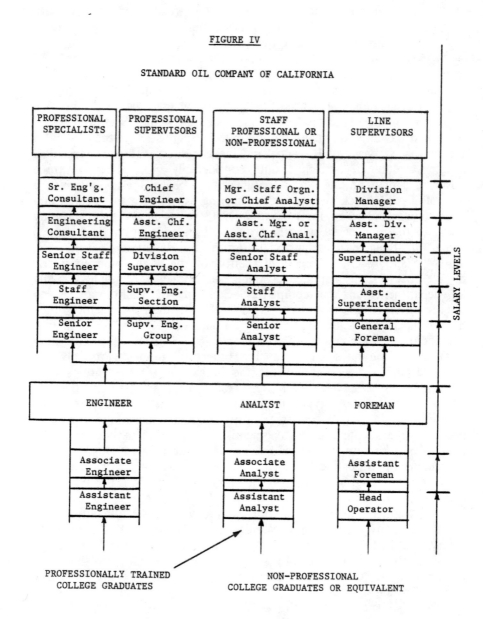

PROFESSIONALLY TRAINED
COLLEGE GRADUATES

NON-PROFESSIONAL
COLLEGE GRADUATES OR EQUIVALENT

1. They found that the scientists and engineers actually saw themselves as performing distinctly different functions from each other and neither group wanted to be lost in the category of the other. Therefore, the clear distinction was made between engineers and scientists.

2. They found that the specific title conferred at each level of progress was very meaningful not only within the laboratory in the company and community but also the world at large. Therefore, great care was taken to assure that the title at every level for each track, was representative of actual duties performed, and of the prestige level.

3. They found that other companies which had failed with the double-track system had not observed a careful monetary compensation level horizontally across all the ladders. Compensation simply was not as high on the technical ladder as on the comparable managerial ladder. Therefore PPG took steps to assure that this equivalency was observed throughout.

4. PPG took pains to assure that the technical ladder could not be used as a dumping ground for scientific has-beens or hacks. Poor selection of personnel could rapidly detract from or demoralize professional image and standards. Technical staff members must be eminently qualified to fill positions in the technical ladder just as is expected of those on the management ladder.

5. Great care was taken in assigning people to the positions in the newly established multiple paths program. Actual individual assignments were extended over a period of two years. The objective was to keep standards high and rising.

6. They found that other companies had sometimes failed with the dual ladder concept because individuals assigned to the professional ladder, especially at the upper levels, had been given consultant type roles only. This seemed to have degenerated rather quickly to the point where the incumbents were becoming increasingly isolated from the organization and sterile in their efforts. PPG preserved the notion of "practicing engineer" and "practicing scientist" permeating the whole ladder from bottom to top. This enabled incumbents in both tracks to continue identifying problems and generating ideas objectively uncovering major technological innovations throughout their entire careers.

7. PPG takes care to assure that an incumbent choosing the manager's track clearly understands that he is now a manager and is no longer performing the functions of the scientist or engineer. The manager who fails to recognize this distinction fails in his job as a manager.

FIGURE V

PPG MULTIPLE PATHS OF PROGRESS PROGRAM

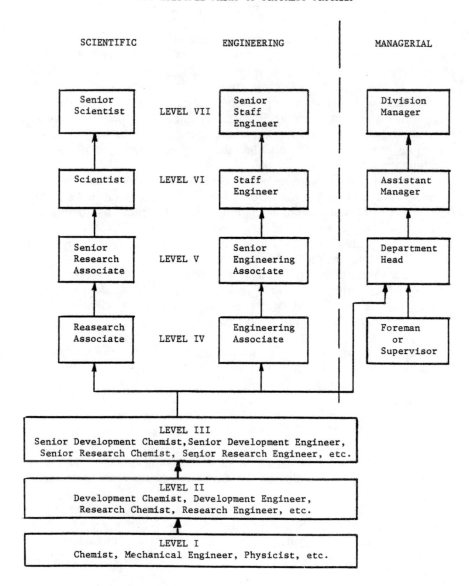

Undoubtedly the most complete, sophisticated, and detailed double-track system that has been studied in this research is that of the Reliance Electric Company of Cleveland, Ohio.   Their double-track system cuts horizontally across every department within the corporation.   A position slotting guide is maintained for all professional, administrative, and technical jobs throughout all departments in the company, and another position slotting guide is maintained for all managerial jobs.   Tieing the two tracks together is a matrix of 27 distinct position levels or pay grades for exempt employees.   Every employee on either ladder can clearly see exactly where his position is in relationship to any other position in the company.   For example the nonsupervisory "senior attorney" can see that he is at grade 23 which is the highest rated professional position in the legal department.   He can also see that the highest rated "general legal attorney" (a management position) would be grade 25 in a division, grade 29 in a group, or grade 30 on a corporate-wide basis. At the same time, the assistant attorney (professional), sees that he is at grade 13 and holding a non-supervisory position.   He can see exactly what professional titled positions exist in the law department, what managerial titled positions exist in the law department, and at exactly what grade each position is classified.   This system provides a means whereby every employee can clearly see what position and compensation is offered in both professional and managerial positions in the company.

CHAPTER 7

CONCLUSIONS FROM THE SURVEY

Limitations Of The Survey

Whenever the researcher sets himself to the task of formally analyzing his research, the bounds and limitations of the research itself seem to become clearly apparent. Some of these limitations will be mentioned here with the hope that the act of evoking them will serve more to clarify than to detract from the ultimate conclusions:

1. In the survey, only "industrial" firms were investigated. By and large, the term "industrial" is equated with "manufacturing." Specifically, all financial institutions, distribution and retailing, transportation, utilities, and educational institutions were excluded from the survey. All of these, particularly the last, are major employers of "professional individual contributors." The scope of the study, and therefore the restrictions of its conclusions, must be borne in mind. In all probability, a number of the conclusions can be applied to the non-industrial sectors, but not on the basis of this study.

2. Another limitation is the fact that the frame of respondents was limited to the 400 largest industrial firms in America (on the basis of annual sales). Even though Table I shows a rapidly diminishing instance of double-track systems as the number of professionals in the firm decreases below 800, the temptation to extrapolate (and conclude that the frequency almost disappears below the largest 400 firms) should probably be resisted. Rather, such a conclusion should wait for validation in a further study.

3. As with any questionnaire, the validity of answers depends upon the individual respondent's interpretation of the questions. For example, even though considerable time and thought were devoted to defining "manager" and "professional" in the questionnaire, apparently the definitions did not totally polarize the mental images of compensation practitioners who may have spent many years working with these terms in a somewhat different context. This is understandable, and may easily represent a flaw in the questionnaire definition rather than in that of the respondent. Likewise, the phrase ". . .two separate

compensation and progression ladders for managers and professionals" (questions 4 and 7) was apparently subject to a rather wide variance of interpretation. This is probably attributable to the paucity of reference in the compensation literature to the "double-track" systems.

4. A few of the largest industrial firms have established separate entities, subsidiaries, or even separate corporations to perform their research functions. Since the double-track is largely a phenomenon of the scientific employee groups, responses to survey questions may have been somewhat misleading from such firms where the research group may not have been considered a part of the "respondent's firm."

Conclusions From The Survey

Conclusions drawn from this survey will be centered on answers to the following six general question areas:

1. To what extent have American industrial firms now adopted double-track systems of compensation?
2. What predictors can be established to characterize companies which now have double-track systems?
3. To which organizational functions (departments) do American industrial firms now apply a double-track compensation system?
4. How high does the professional ladder now go, as compared to the managerial ladder in American firms?
5. To what extent do American firms anticipate the application of a double-track system in the future?
6. Who are the individuals currently considered authorities on compensation of professionals and managers in America today?

1.   Firms Now Having Double-Track Systems

As shown in Table I all respondent firms were listed in rank order according to the number of professionals employed in each company. The company names have not been listed since all respondents were assured anonymity.

The following is a condensation of the totals from Table I as derived from question number four in the questionnaire:

1. Number of firms having *no* double-track   56

2. Number of firms *having* double-tracks in:
    a. Scientific departments plus at least one
        other department function: 16
    b. Scientific department *only*, (R & D
        and/or Engineering):   19
    c. Informal systems (not spelled out):   9

                        TOTAL RESPONDENT FIRMS   100

A total of 44 of the 100 responding companies (44%) indicate some use of double-track systems, though 9 of these are "informal." Nineteen firms indicate use of the double-track in scientific departments only. Sixteen have developed formal systems for departments other than scientific.

TABLE I

ALL FIRMS, BY NUMBER OF PROFESSIONALS

Q1 Number of Managers	Q2 Number of Professionals	Q4 Double-Track?	
		Yes	No
26,000	52,000		X
49,800	31,848		X
18,000	20,000	S	
5,500	15,500	X	
10,377	13,790	I	
4,308	13,179	X	
12,000	10,000	X	
8,000	9,500	X	
2,945	9,218	S	
2,500	9,000	S	
3,345	7,892		X
2,365	7,200		X
6,500	7,000	I	
2,000	7,000	I	
4,500	6,000	X	
2,000	6,000		X
6,000	6,000	X	
15,500	5,400	S	

TABLE I (Cont.)

ALL FIRMS, BY NUMBER OF PROFESSIONALS

Q1 Number of Managers	Q2 Number of Professionals	Q4 Double-Track?	
		Yes	No
1,000	5,000	X	
2,000	5,000	X	
900	5,000	S	
13,453	4,732		X
5,075	4,050	S	
1,200	4,000	I	
5,334	3,656		X
1,076	3,388	S	
3,880	3,140		X
3,972	3,082		X
950	3,000	S	
2,500	3,000	X	
1,267	2,700	S	
3,000	2,600	X	
2,500	2,500		X
2,600	2,500	I	
1,600	2,400		X
2,000	2,000		X
3,500	2,000	S	
1,805	1,820	S	
2,800	1,806	S	
1,445	1,785	S	
3,500	1,700	S	
990	1,590	X	
600	1,500	X	
5,200	1,500	S	
2,000	1,500	I	
3,203	1,333		X
3,246	1,083		X
1,403	1,012	X	
2,500	1,000		X
1,500	1,000	S	
2,800	1,000		X
1,000	1,000		X

TABLE I (Cont.)

ALL FIRMS, BY NUMBER OF PROFESSIONALS

Q1 Number of Managers	Q2 Number of Professionals	Q4 Double-Track? Yes	No
675	963	S	
3,464	951		X
1,400	900	I	
1,200	900		X
935	889		X
1,655	868	X	
284	816		X
1,400	800		X
1,544	797	X	
1,338	765		X
1,500	700		X
1,500	600		X
1,380	594		X
2,000	500		X
800	500	S	
530	500	S	
250	500		X
135	450		X
1,232	398		X
960	365		X
990	350		X
569	301	I	
700	300	I	
1,000	300		X
1,430	300		X
3,700	300		X
416	278		X
240	260		X
900	250		X
550	250		X
1,150	220	X	
304	211		X
2,000	200		X
500	200		X

TABLE I (Cont.)

ALL FIRMS, BY NUMBER OF PROFESSIONALS

Q1 Number of Managers	Q2 Number of Professionals	Q4 Double-Track? Yes	No
1,000	150		X
700	150		X
45	140		X
475	125		X
1,400	100		X
800	100		X
1,500	100		X
134	92		X
249	48		X
520	30		X
36	15		X

Key: X   Yes or No
      S   Scientific departments only
      I   Informal Double-Track system (not spelled out)

2.   Predictors of Companies Now Having Double-Track Systems

From the data of Table I it can be seen that as the number of professionals in a firm decreases, so the probability decreases that the firm may have a double-track system. In those companies having 1,000 or more professional employees, 71% of them have some type of double-track system though it may embrace only the scientific departments, or may be only an informal system.

With only one exception, no respondent firm employing less than 797 professional employees has a formal company-wide double-track system. From this it can be concluded that, at the present time, there appears to be a cutoff point at about 800 professional employees below which companies have not found it feasible to employ double-track compensation and progression systems on a company-wide basis.

All respondent companies were grouped according to industries by use of Standard Industrial Code (SIC) Numbers. Since many companies overlap two or more industries, each company was listed according to the first-mentioned SIC Number as given in the Dunn and Bradstreet Million Dollar Directory. The results are shown in Table II.

Industries are rank-ordered from high to low according to the proportion of companies employing the double-track system.

From Table II it can be seen that all five respondent firms which are in the business of manufacturing Photographic, Measuring, and Control Devices (SIC 38), now have Double-Track systems. At the opposite extreme, companies having no double-track systems were in the industries producing Fabricated Metal Products, Textiles, Tobacco, Rubber and Plastics (SIC 21, 22, 30, 34).

TABLE II

Number of Companies Using Double-Track Systems--by SIC Number (Industry)

SIC #		Use D-T? Yes	No	% Using
38	Photographic, measuring & control instruments	5	0	100%
28	Pharmaceuticals (only)	4	1	80%
32	Glass, clay, stone, concrete products	5	2	71.5%
13, 29	Gas & petroleum extracting, re-fining, & chemicals (other than pharmaceuticals)	8	6	57%
37, 35	Transportation equipment & non-electrical machinery	12	12	50%
36	Electrical & electronic machinery	3	5	37.5%
33	Primary metals	3	7	30%
24, 26	Lumber, wood, paper, & allied products	3	9	25%
20	Food products	1	6	14%
21, 22, 30, 34	Fabricated metal products, textiles, tobacco, rubber, & plastics	0	8	0
	TOTAL	44	56	44%

3. To Which Departments are Firms Applying Double-Track Systems?

Table III shows the departments in which respondent firms now apply double-track ladders. Notable is the fact that just two firms, of the one hundred respondents, employ a double-track system through all eleven of the typical company departments listed in the table. After the scientific departments, Marketing is the next most common department in which the systems prevail, with Data Processing/Systems departments next in order.

4. How High Can the Professional Progress as Compared to the Manager?

In responding to survey question number six (Does the professional in your firm have the possibility of reaching a compensation level which is second only to that of your chief executive?), 24 of the 100 respondents answered in the affirmative. However, just four of these respondents were those which do have a formal double-track system throughout their companies. Presumably the remaining 20 companies have some type of job evaluation system which theoretically provides for the non-supervising professional to reach the number two position in the company.

Of the 24 companies indicating that it is possible for the professional to reach the number two position in the company, nine of them indicated that nobody in their firm had actually ever done so (answered "no" to question 6b). This left 15 firms indicating that it was not only possible for the professional to reach the number two position but that it actually had been done. The telephone survey of these 15 companies indicated that the question hinged upon a literal interpretation of the word "professional." In each company, the individual reaching the number two spot, had pursued a career which was essentially "professional," in that he had devoted the majority of his career to specialized pursuits as an individual contributor. However, in every one of the 15 cases, it was elicited that the incumbent had, at some point in his career, actually "crossed-over" and performed as a "manager" before reaching the number two position.

It was interesting to note that three companies answered that it is impossible for the professional to reach the number two position but, nevertheless, somebody *had* done so. In these three cases the feat had been performed by an internationally recognized scientist on the order of Steinmetz, Edison, or Land.

TABLE III

RESPONDENT FIRMS HAVE DOUBLE TRACK SYSTEMS IN THE
DEPARTMENTS INDICATED

Company Identification	Research & Development	Engineering	Marketing	E.D.P./Systems	Industrial Eng'g.	Legal	Accounting	Finance	Ind'l. Relations	Purchasing	Prod., Inv. Control
A	X	X	X	X	X	X	X	X	X	X	X
B	X	X	X	X	X	X	X	X	X	X	X
C	X	X	X	X	X	X	X	X	X	X	
D	X	X	X	X	X		X	X	X	X	
E	X	X	X			X	X	X			X
F	X	X	X	X	X		X	X			
G	X	X		X	X	X		X			
H	X	X		X	X	X	X		X		
I	X	X	X	X					X		
J	X	X				X					
K	X	X		X							
L	X	X	X								
M	X	X	X		X						
N	X	X		X							
O	X	X	X			X					
P	X	X	X								
Totals	16	16	11	10	8	8	7	7	6	4	3
Scientific	19	19									
Grand Totals	35	35	11	10	8	8	7	7	6	4	3

In answering question 6a (How high does the professional ladder go compared to that of your chief executive?), respondents replied in several different ways. The two most common approaches to answering the question are tabulated in Table IV; expressed respectively as a percentage of the chief executive officer's salary, and in terms of organization levels counting the CEO as level number one.

TABLE IV

How High Can the Professional Progress Compared to the CEO?

Expressed as % of CEO's Pay		Expressed in "Levels," Counting CEO as Level #1	
No. of Co's Responding	% of CEO's Salary	No. of Co's Responding	Status or Pay Level
1	65%	6	3
1	60%	8	4
1	33%	3	5
4	30%	3	6
4	25%	1	10
1	20%	1	11
1	17%	2	12
3	15%	1	16
1	10%		
17		25	

When expressed in terms of the CEO's compensation, it appears that the professional's maximum compensation can vary from a low of 10% of the CEO's compensation in one company to as much as 65% in another company. However, a clear mode emerges indicating that 25-30% of the CEO's compensation would be the maximum expected compensation for the professional.

In terms of "levels" the interpretation would largely depend upon that one company's salary and hierarchical structure, and have some direct relation to span of control and decentralization within the organization. However, the mode clearly appears to be at the third or fourth level of the organization. It should be pointed out, that the 24 companies answering that the professional can actually reach the second level (answered "yes" to question 6) have not been included in the tabulation of Table IV for the reasons explained above.

The maximum level attainable for the professional was also expressed in several other ways. Three respondents expressed it in terms of a proportion of all salaried people.   Two indicated that the professional can reach the top 10% of salaried persons, while the third indicated he can reach the top 5% of all salaried people.

Three other respondents expressed the professional's maximum in terms of direct annual salary.   One indicated a top maximum salary of $60,00 a year, a second indicated a top of $45,000 a year, while a third indicated $46,500 per year.

The remaining respondents, who answered question 6a, have the following phrases to indicate the maximum level attainable for the professional:

> Two indicated "equal to the highest administrative function in his own department."

> Two indicated "a position equal to middle management."

> One said "equal to a director."

> One said "equal to a division vice president."

> One said "equal to a department manager."

> One said "less than half of the CEO's compensation level."

It is important to reemphasize that correspondents answered question 6a (How high does the professional ladder go compared to that of your chief executive?), by the use of numerous frames of reference such as:

> a.   % of CEO's salary.
> b.   How many "organizational levels" below the CEO?
> c.   Proportion of total salaried people in the company.
> d.   Direct annual salary figures.
> e.   In terms of the professional's own department manager.
> f.   In terms of titles (Director, or Vice Pres., etc.)

In analyzing results of question 6a, care was taken to avoid attempting to correlate the answers from one frame of reference with those of another.

It was enlightening to observe the many varied frames of reference by which compensation practitioners describe a given compensation level. This suggests the possibility that much can be done in the future to increase communication between professional compensation people, and to codify standard terminology and quantitative reference scales.

5. The Future Use of Double-Track Systems

Question number seven, by definition, was to be answered only by the 56 respondents who indicated they now have no double-track ladder of any kind. Of these 56, just six indicated that they now foresee the possibility of the use of a double-track system within the next few years. Five of the six indicated that some form of a double-track system is already in the planning or evaluation stage for use in their company. However, this response leaves the clear inference that there is definitely not a *perceived* need for a double-track system in those companies not now having them.

6. Who are the Current Experts in the Compensation Field Today?

Responses to question number eight in the survey generated a total list of 38 names. Two names received eight mentions, the highest plurality of any:

> Robert S. Sibson of Sibson & Co.
> Kenneth E. Foster of Towers, Perrin, Forster & Crosby, Inc. (T.P.F. & C.) (formerly with Xerox)

Next in order, with five mentions, came the name of Graef S. Crystal, also of T.P.F. & C. The following 12 names were mentioned by two respondents each:

> Bruce R. Ellig—Pfizer, Inc.
> George H. Foote—McKinsey & Co.
> Lloyd E. Fuller—Sandia Corp.
> Conrad C. Greim—Whirlpool Corp.
> H. B. Guerci—Bell Laboratories
> Arthur A. Handy, Jr—Kaiser Industries
> Richard G. Jamison—Rockwell International
> Fran W. Miller—Honeywell, Inc.
> James F. Moore—Exxon Corp.
> Milton Rock—Hay Assoc.
> Richard Wing—Eastman Kodak
> Donald G. Winton—Reliance Electric

Twenty-three other names were mentioned just once each. These names will not be listed since a single mention would appear to carry very questionable statistical weight. The wide field mentioned however, would infer the clear indication, that among compensation practitioners, there is definitely not a polarization of opinion with regard to the leaders in their field.

CHAPTER 8

IMPLICATIONS FOR THE FUTURE

It has been demonstrated in this paper that professionals represent a distinct and significant group in American industry which is continually increasing in size. Rosow estimates that there are well over 10 million professionals in industry today. He states that "in the past, professionals were a select group who were a very small proportion of the total organization—now, they may be *the* organization, and they are the greatest single investment in manpower. The terms 'burden,' 'overhead,' and 'staff' are outmoded in today's organization. Professionals are no longer the dependent luxury group who enjoyed a certain status but were of uncertain value to the organization."[1]

The research of this paper has shown that the majority of American industrial firms do not, at the present time, recognize a distinct ladder of compensation and progression for the professional parallel to, and in any way equal to, that of the manager. It has further been shown that in those companies which do not now have any kind of double-track system, the vast majority do not anticipate moving to any such system in the next few years.

There is even an element of definite opposition to the use of double-track systems as demonstrated by some of the observations given in Appendix A.

In analyzing the future implications of the conclusions drawn in Chapter 7, the same question areas will be taken up in the same order as taken in that chapter:

1. Firms Now Having Double-Track Systems

Less than half of the respondent firms indicate any use of formal double-track system, or even any anticipation of its future use. Two possible lines of reasoning suggest themselves for those companies which do not anticipate use of the double-track:

    a. Company management does not perceive there to be any critical difference between the factors of compensation sought by the professionals versus those factors sought by managers. Hence, a single integrated system will suffice their company in the foreseeable future.

    b. Company management does not see the future need for professionals in any greater quantity or quality than are now being recruited and retained through their present methods.

Their personnel needs will be filled without providing any further financial or progression inducements for professionals, and without providing any means to dissuade professionals from seeking management positions.

Both of the above lines of reasoning may be entirely valid in cases of individual companies. However, if a firm anticipates a need for increasing numbers of professionals, with increasing levels of expertise, it is axiomatical that some means must be developed to attract, recruit, motivate, and retain the increasing corps of superior professionals. A double-track system, by definition, provides such a means.

Let us picture a new college graduate being considered for employment by a company. He will have many questions occurring to him, but among the first he will want to know: (a) where he can progress within the organization, (b) how much he will be paid for his work, and (c) what will be expected of him. A double-track system should help to answer these questions and should, therefore, have a marked influence on the recruitment, interviewing, and placement of the new employee. It should provide a graphic map showing him the levels of compensation available to him given the alternatives between managerial and professional positions. It could help to avoid the negative effects of misdirection and misgivings so common to the neophyte in business.

Later in his career, the double-track system would serve as a guide and reference to which he could relate his changing set of needs, objectives, and ambitions. At this point, he would be in a position to consider his total current accomplishments within the organization. The degree of his personal motivation would be another factor of consideration. All of these factors would be brought together in bringing his career plan up-to-date.

It is difficult to believe that any company would have a professional development program which does not include a clear picture of the compensation available to the incumbent at each level of progression, and in each of the various career avenues available to him. Important in this concept is an insight to the *comparative* compensation between the professional and his counterpart on the managerial track. A double-track system can provide these necessary bench marks for both managers and professionals. The use of the double-track should tend to minimize the high company expense which is the consequence of the inefficient use of manpower, and the misdirection of individual career plans.

From the above discussion, these two general policy questions seem to present themselves to the American industrial firm of today:

1.   Is it appropriate or necessary for a firm to create two or more separate sets of criteria by which employees are to be compensated and by which they are to evaluate their career progress?   Is the "manager" enough different from the "professional" in his wants, talents, values,and temperament to warrant such a double standard?

     The firms which have adopted double-track systems have demonstrated their preference for exercising this double standard.   On the other hand, users of a single integrated position evaluation plan, such as the Hay Guide Charts, seem to deny the need for separate evaluations of managers and professionals.

2.   Ideologically, should the professional's compensation be as high as that of the manager or possibly even higher?   Is the manager's value to the company generally higher than that of the professional?   Does the professional's presumed greater education, training, and preparation warrant an even higher compensation than that of the manager or is the manager's coordination of company resources more valuable to the firm than the professional's expertise?

George H. Foote has made the provocative observation (Appendix B), that in Germany top professionals tend to be paid more than the top managers, in contrast to general practice in America which is the reverse.

It is not the purpose of this research to answer these questions which are inevitably faced by every company.   Rather, it is the purpose of this paper to define and describe one approach to the problems of attracting, retaining, and developing an effective corps of professionals; a double-track system.   Also, it is the purpose, here, to evaluate the present use of double-tracks in this country and to predict its future use.

Accepting the fact that any given employee's level of compensation is ultimately the result of bargaining between the employer and employee (Chapter 3), it is not suggested that a double-track system can ever actually *set* a given employee's compensation level (any more than compensation levels are ever actually *set* by job evaluation).   Rather, it is suggested that a double-track system is one means for giving validity and perspective to a company's compensation structure.   In so doing, it can be hoped that the double-track can be one more tool for attracting, career planning, retaining, and motivating employees to the optimum accomplishment of company goals.

In visualizing the double-track system, it might be well to consider the extension of the professional track downward to include paraprofessionals, specialists, technicians, etc., whose "advanced knowledge in a field of science or learning" differs from that of the professional only in degree. It must be assumed that the paraprofessional, specialist, and technician are human beings subject to ambitions, wants, and needs for status and job satisfaction just as are professionals. It may be that the professional ladder ought to be extended downward to include the above employees just as the managerial ladder is assumed to reach down to the first line supervisors.

2.   Predictors of Companies Having Double-Track Systems

The predictors developed in Chapter 7 may provide some useful guidelines to company managers when comparing their own company policies and trends with those of similar companies and competitors.

From Table I (Chapter 7) it becomes apparent that any company with more than 800 professional employees should give serious consideration to the possible attributes of a double-track system, if they have not already done so. If the company has more than 1,000 professionals, they should be aware that almost 3 out of every 4 companies having as many professionals have already adopted such a system in at least their scientific departments. Likewise, any company with more than 500 professional employees might be well-advised to examine the use of a double-track for at least their scientific departments.

Table II (Chapter 7) gives some clear indicators for industrial managers, since the right hand column represents the statistical probability of a double-track system existing in each group of industries named. (Note that all figures in this research represent a 25% sampling of all American industrial firms in Fortune's top 400 with respect to annual sales.)

From the simple standpoint of inter-company competition, as firms seek to recruit, motivate, and retain professional employees, they must inevitably concern themselves with any technique which has successfully implemented those functions for their competitors.

3.   In Which Departments are Double-Track Systems Being Applied?

From Table III it is apparent that the system of double-track is a phenomenon of the scientific departments, first and foremost. (This reference normally indicating Research, Development, and/or Engineering.) Of the 35 respondent firms now employing a formal double-track system, all of them apply it to the scientific departments, while 19 of them (54%) apply it *only* in their scientific departments.

This data provides the clear indication that any firm considering the use of the double-track should begin with the scientific departments. A number of respondents indicated that their scientific departments included the majority of the professionals in their companies. Conceptually, it would appear that firms will naturally tend to provide compensation and progression inducements where the need seems greatest, and the numbers of employees are the greatest. This rather obvious philosophy not only gives credence to the idea of applying the double-track first to the scientific departments, but it also suggests that, as numbers of professionals increase in other departments, the double-track will tend to be applied to those departments.

4.   The Upper Limits of the Two Tracks

The conclusion was clearly drawn in Chapter 7 that the direct monetary upper limit of the professional ladder appears to be about 25% to 30% of the dollar compensation value of the managerial ladder at its upper limit. The converse of this statement is that the maximum total compensation of the highest manager (CEO), is at least three times that of the highest professional.

This may represent one of the most alarming signals to be drawn from the data of the present research. It suggests a number of questions which must be faced by industrial managers, such as:

a. If the entering professional employee is aware that his maximum potential monetary compensation in this firm will be only one third that of a managerial employee, will he be happy to join the firm, continue to be motivated to optimum performance, and remain with the firm throughout his career?

b. If the entering employee is *not* aware of the wide spread in monetary potential between the two tracks, will he become demoralized at a later date, upon discovering the truth?

c. Knowing of the wide potential spread, will the entering employee want to know what factors in his total compensation package will justify and make up for the difference in money?

Practitioners of Compensation are charged with providing answers to questions such as these. A double-track system is a method of describing the comparative potentials of the manager's track and the professional's track, each track being laid out to provide the factors of compensation which will motivate the particular followers of that track.

5.   The Future Use of Double-Track Systems

It has been demonstrated in the previous chapter that those practitioners of compensation who are not now using a double-track system, clearly do not anticipate a general movement to its use in the foreseeable future. However, certain conditions and forecasts cannot be ignored:

The increasingly expanding and accelerating store of human knowledge, in every avenue of endeavor, has been popularly dramatized by Alvin Toffler in his "Future Shock." Toffler's statements such as the following, have demonstrated the obvious conclusion that everyone, in his work, must become more and more a specialist, and continually become more expert in his particular technology: "Ninety percent of all scientists who ever lived are still alive," or "There are more scientists on the faculty of Georgia Tech, today, than there were in the entire world in 1900," or "Since the beginning of this century, more than 60% has been slashed from the average time needed for a major scientific discovery to be translated into useful technological form," or "Output of books in the world has now exceeded 1,000 titles per day," or "Scientific and technical literature mounts at the rate of 60 million pages per year," and finally, "The report of the new knowledge discovered *each day* of the year would fill an entire Encyclopedia Britannica."

It can hardly be denied that every professional must inevitably learn more and more about his own profession simply to remain a viable unit in an organization. From this, it can only be concluded that the professional cannot be expected to achieve expertise in a totally different field (the field of management) than his own particular specialty. It seems inevitably to follow, therefore, that companies must increasingly, in the future, provide some means for motivating their professionals without diluting the professional's endeavors by requiring that he learn and practice the art or science of management.

With respect to controlling the behavior of the professional, a simple logic sequence suggests itself:

1.   Professionals must be motivated by the assurance that their compensation will, in some measure, be commensurate with other employees in their company (managers) who have similar education and industrial experience, and who exert similar mental effort.

2.   Every employee's compensation must be paid in terms of his own specific desires and needs for fulfillment.

3.   The sum total of knowledge in every profession is increasing at a continually accelerating pace, requiring ever greater personal study and self-development.

4. The clear limits of the human being will prevent any professional from maintaining current superior expertise in his profession while simultaneously achieving expertise in a totally unrelated profession; the profession of managing people and resources.

5. Just as the individual must make the choice between the two diverse approaches to his profession, so the company must design a compensation package to motivate the employee along the particular path which he has chosen (or the company has chosen for him).

The above leads to another implication for the future to be suggested by the author. It is not one which has been reached by a pragmatic data analysis leading to a mechanical conclusion. Rather, it has been suggested by personal study of the compensation field previous to, and coincident with the process of data collection and analysis: There should be, and will be a pronounced increase in the definition and the use of double-track systems of compensation and progression in industrial firms in this country in the next few years.

One final generalization seems to emerge from this study: It appears that much effort is currently being devoted, in this country, to making extensive "salary surveys," "executive compensation surveys," and "CEO compensation surveys," so that "companies may know what others are paying for given positions." However, much less effort seems to be devoted to disseminating information and experience with "techniques" of compensation administration The latter seems a fertile area for renewed endeavor to the benefit of all organizations.

Recommendations For Further Study

This study has focused upon large American industrial firms, and suggests a wide array of companion studies on comparative compensation between managers and individual contributors. In particular, educational institutions might benefit from an investigation of compensation comparisons; where the number of professionals greatly exceeds the number of managers (administrators), and where the compensation spread between the two ladders is presumably much smaller than in industry. Also, as suggested by the example of the U.S. Agriculture Research Service outlined in this study, certain governmental agencies could easily benefit from comparative compensation studies; so too, financial institutions, utilities, marketing and advertising agencies, etc.

Another possibility has been suggested by George H. Foote (appendix), in stating that the professional ladder in German firms traditionally extends higher than the managerial ladder, while the reverse is true in American enterprises. A comparative international study could throw light upon the characteristics causing this difference.

Surveys of compensation "levels" for specific positions and industries, so common in today's business community, have the disadvantage of the continual dynamic influence of changes in the general economy. Therefore, comparative compensation studies, of which this is an example, would seem to have the advantage of more permanent, useful indicators for compensation design not provided by "levels" studies.

Since this study surveyed only the largest 400 industrial firms in the country, a further study could extend to a population including considerably smaller firms. Such a study could validate the inference that very few double-track systems exist in smaller firms, which could lead to the conclusion that there is an exceedingly low incidence of the systems in American industry as a whole, today.

NOTES

[1]Jerome M. Rosow, *Management Record,* XXIV, No. 2, February, 1962, p. 20.

APPENDIX A

This appendix includes some of the typical voluntary comments made by compensation practitioners regarding the use of the double-track system. These quotations were gleaned from the responses to survey question No. 4, also from correspondence between the author and respondents, and from personal interviews made either by telephone or in person.

Comments generally unfavorable to the double-track system are listed first, followed by generally favorable comments, concluding with warnings by two authorities regarding the judicious and selective use of the double-track.

From a wood products company:

> "I doubt that separate schedules or bases for compensating managers and professionals serves a useful purpose from a corporate management standpoint."

From a manufacturer of glass and insulation:

> "Don't feel the dual ladder concept has a place as such in business. It is an artificial and academic distinction. Business should only ask: Is the job necessary and what is competitive pay for the job? It does not matter whether it happens to be managerial or professional, or a combination of both, which is so often found."

From a paper products firm:

> "The professional ladder has a limited application in research and development functions or in *certain* staff functions which are *not oriented* to operating tasks or functions. The professional ladder can be a very negative development harness."

From a textile firm:

> "The distinction between 'managers' and 'professionals' is not a valid one in my view. In my experience most industries do not make this distinction and remuneration and promotion are based only on ability and experience."

From a pharmaceutical firm:

> "At one time we had a dual ladder in research, but it was integrated because for us it was artificial. In many cases it was contradictory to our job evaluation system."

From an oil company:

> "Our compensation policies and programs are flexible enough to accommodate 'good human resource needs and actions.' Programs don't pay people right. Good management does. Separate ladders and/or procedures mean nothing unless there is tangible visible evidence of same. We have demonstrated by example."

From a machinery manufacturer:

> "We do not plan, nor do we have any expectation of the need, to formulate separate compensation structures. In our opinion there is no more need for a separation of compensation structures for professionals and managers than exists for managers and executives. In fact, such a separation could be highly undesirable in that it could provoke more dissatisfaction than favorable reaction. In my judgment, our high level professionals have little if any doubt about how the compensation levels for their positions compare with the compensation levels of other positions, including many of the positions in management."

From an auto manufacturer:

> "The dual ladder can be a dumping ground for professionals who are not superior professionals or managers. In many companies these are the resting places for professionals who have not kept up with their field and who can't handle the tougher managerial assignments."

From another pharmaceutical firm:

> "Our ladder is currently under revision. The ladder will deteriorate if it's not managed equitably on a continuous basis. It can easily become a "status" club serving a very limited need."

In contrast to the above generally negative comments the following are representative of those comments from practitioners who have favorable feelings towards double-track systems:

From an oil company:

> "We have used separate ladders for 17 years and believe it is both equitable and an effective utilization of manpower."

From a manufacturer of transportation equipment:

> "What we call the 'dual ladder of progression' has been a general philosophy of our company for many years. Recently it has

fallen into general misuse due to swings of unemployment and inflationary conditions. Work progresses here regarding a cleanup or redefinition. I personally believe that the concept has greater merit today than it did 20 years ago, when one considers the aversion some employees have to joining the management ladder race."

From a steel company:

"There is need, in my opinion, for the dual ladder. Fortunately, our single classification allows for (although not formally recognizing) this need. It is, however, an area that needs a great deal of further study and I am pleased to see that your survey zeros in on even more specifics in this 'never-never land.'"

From an electrical and electronics equipment manufacturer:

"Recently I have proposed a compensation ladder equating salary levels and standardizing titles on each ladder; the professional versus managerial. It seems appropriate and should be pursued as published policy and disseminated to promote professional motivation within the companies and on the campus."

From a machinery conglomerate:

"The dual ladder is becoming more prevalent and necessary in order to recognize individual ability and contribution and still maintain a distinction between the 'policy maker' and the 'professional.' In addition, the ability to recognize ability and contributions without the necessity of 'promoting' a non-manager into a position which has primary administrative and motivational components."

From a producer of building materials:

"All salaried positions are written and evaluated. All employees are aware of the fact that dual ladders of progression do exist, but in all fields, the managerial ladder goes to a higher grade level. Each profession has its own dual ladder."

From a food company:

"We are a manufacturing and marketing company offering supervisory and management positions in all areas. The dual ladder is important in a technical company where management positions are not available or desirable for certain employees."

From another foods processor:

> "'Force fitting' professional positions into the same salary
> ranges with administrative and management positions has caused little
> problems up to three years ago. Most critical area now, in our food
> company, is in the engineering field. Attraction and retention of
> qualified personnel increasing is becoming more difficult."

From a manufacturer of measuring and control instruments:

> "I believe most technically oriented companies, such as
> ours, provide the opportunity for the individual contributor to reach
> rather high levels of compensation without opting to the managerial
> positions."

The following comments made by Harry P. Knox of
Addressograph-Multigraph Corporation comprise a neutral, if judicial,
warning with regard to both sides of the double-track ladder:

> "There may be great danger in easing the way for
> professionals to ascend as non-managers. Most professionals become
> valuable to business only as they are forced to think and act like
> managers—as well as—independent 'experts.' The person valued for
> specialized knowledge and degrees too often becomes a liability by
> working at purposes in conflict with integrated management goals.
> There are too many 'degree duds' who ask to be valued
> for their diplomas, rugged individualism and 'years of experience'
> since degree (pure socialism).
> Yet, many outstanding specialists with or without degree
> are under-valued by action-oriented management types who ascend
> by avoidance of anything complicated.
> Describing and evaluating business positions is weakened
> critically by the lack of reference information of functions to be
> performed within business. Business failures could be reduced and
> profits multiplied if better academic information were put in more
> usable form defining functio s and subfunctions to be managed,
> diagramming preferred organization structure and best alternatives.
> Businesses suffer gross inefficiencies, duplications, and
> conflicts because the decision-level doers refuse the time and patience
> to 'sort out' functions. And the 'thinkers' have failed to produce
> graphically clear charts, tables, and diagrams showing the way to
> more effective, less costly 'functioning' of the labors primary to
> business success."

The following comments were made by Herbert Messer of
Republic Steel Corporation in urging caution in the application of the
double-track system specifically in the steel industry. Mr. Messer says:

"As you may be aware the steel industry employs a sizable number of individuals with degrees in the specialized area of science, for example metallurgists. Some of our metallurgists at some point in their careers may be assigned to a research department. In that capacity they may or may not devote a substantial part of their time to directing the work of other people since our research units are often organized in the project. Further, metallurgists are frequently transferred to our operating districts and divisions and in some cases are assigned to operating positions. Accordingly, it becomes very difficult, without doing an individual case by case analysis, to determine if the metallurgist is at the moment a professional or a manager or both at a given point in time.

In our salaried administration program they have not established a separate formal professional ladder. In both systems, however, we do have a limited professional ladder built into the classification programs. For example, an attorney may progress up five steps in salary grade without assuming managerial responsibilities. These salary grade assignments are based on experience and, more importantly, the degree on difficulty of the legal work performed. The difficulty is in determining at what point an attorney crosses the threshold from being purely a professional and where we would count him as a manager.

I doubt very much that we would attempt to have two separate compensation and profession ladders for managers and professionals in our corporation in the near future. The administrative burdens of making these determinations, particularly in a constantly changing organizational environment would in my opinion, be excessive and outweigh the potential benefits.

In my experience, corporations which have done the greatest amount of work on developing separate compensation and progression ladders are those industries which are characterized by having first, a substantial number of employees engaged in research and development activities and, secondly, use relatively few employees with professional training in the operating end of their business. It is much easier in that kind of a company to sort out who should be compensated on a professional ladder and who should be compensated on a managerial ladder. Further, the transfer of professionals to managerial positions and vice versa tends to be limited, which reduces the administrative problems involved with such transfers."

APPENDIX B

This appendix includes statements by three compensation authorities with regard to the specific factors which ought to be considered in the compensation of professionals as differentiated from the compensation of managers.

Recommendations of James F. Moore, Exxon Corp.:

WHAT FACTORS OUGHT TO BE CONSIDERED IN ESTAB-LISHING THE COMPENSATION OF A PROFESSIONAL AND WHY?

WHAT FACTORS OUGHT TO BE USED WITH RESPECT TO A MANAGER? WHY?

It seems that the starting point to answer the above two questions is to recognize there are a number of factors common to both professional and manager positions. This perspective helps to better identify the differences in the positions filled by employees who most often have the same academic backgrounds, have a common starting point in the company and have a high degree of success within their organization. The following common factors assume that the professional has achieved considerable success and is at the top of the professional ladder.

Common Factors

a. Sets high personal performance standards; is objective
b. Good organizer--knows how to approach problems, formulate, explore, conduct work, analyze
c. Draws sound conclusions, arrives at significant recommendations
d. Sells results of work by good writing and speaking
e. Has ability on most difficult problems to explain, debate, find holes

It would seem that the following factors set the professional and manager positions apart:

Professional Factors

a.   Excellent knowledge of his profession
b.   Personal growth largely dependent on self in staying abreast of latest trends/developments in his profession
c.   Moves his profession within the company to deeper understanding and sphere of influence e.g., greater sales, improved accounting procedures to enhance profits, advanced technological applications.
d.   Attracts most difficult problems in his profession; considered by management as one of the experts if not "the expert"
e.   Writes company reports, memoranda, publications that are source material for others
f.   Has respect of peers for his professional qualifications
g.   Respected member of professional society, top professional should be sought by professional society to consult on special problems, serve on committees, make talks, and serve on panels
h.   Ability to take proper amount of time to consider all necessary factors of problem, to know when results of study should be expanded or when it may be time to "throw in the towel" because of diminishing returns

Management Factors

a.   Good knowledge of his profession
b.   Personal growth dependent on ability to supervise others and sell their output to management
c.   Moves his organization to broader horizons in company, exerting more influence, attracting attention of higher levels of management or other related functions
d.   Sought out to get volume of work done by others in most efficient and economical way
e.   Plans, reports on status of work, prepares budgets, administers employee programs
f.   Has respect of professionals for his ability to manage function
g.   Respected member of management team
h.   Emotional stability
i.   Ability to delegate to others
j.   High degree of cost consciousness
k.   Particularly mindful of strategies, broad implications, the politics of the situation

l. Good communicator--up, down and sideways

m. Willing to shoulder responsibility and make personal sacrificies to progress in company

If these are the essential factors for the top level positions on the two ladders how then do you evaluate them to arrive at the worth of one job relative to the other? To weigh the importance of these dissimilar factors seems most difficult. Even if it could be done, it would be a highly subjective exercise that would probably not lead to a universally satisfactory answer in any organization.

The most practical approach to establish the compensation levels for the top of each ladder is to determine as well as possible what is being paid for work of a similar nature in competitive companies, other industrial companies and other organizations such as public accounting firms (for controller's positions), banks and investment houses (for treasurer's positions), engineering contractors (for engineering positions),etc. It may also be helpful to compare the level of the top professional's salary with professor salaries as professionals so often consider themselves on a par with them and are vulnerable to leave for academic positions. (This may be difficult to do because of the differences in working hours that allows consulting income by the professors.) Comparability of high level professional jobs will be difficult at best because of varying job demands and abilities of incumbents but conscientious judgments coupled with what management believes is appropriate in terms of the overall needs of the organization seems to be the best route to establish top compensation levels.

To establish the lower level professional positions, it would seem advisable to take into consideration (1) starting salaries of each profession, (2) percentile salaries that are normally paid in each profession (data from surveys, etc.) and (3) the compensation for the top level professional covered previously to form an integrated ladder.

Assuming competitive data is available to establish compensation levels for professional ladders of five to eight steps it should be borne in mind that the sky may be the limit to pay that unique individual who has truly made a name for the corporation. Such an occasion occurs very infrequently but if it does, it should be recognized as an inordinate step on any professional ladder. In essence it is an addendum to the ladder for the extraordinary person rather than a realistically attainable step to be filled by the best professional regardless of his capabilities.

WHAT FACTORS OUGHT TO BE CONSIDERED IN ESTABLISHING THE STATUS OF A PROFESSIONAL?

a. Company-wide announcement of promotions
b. Community-wide announcement of promotions
c. Attendance at high level company meetings
d. Payment of professional society memberships
e. Regular attendance at professional society meetings
f. Office appointment comparable to those of the manager or supervisors at a slightly lower level
g. Personalized stationery
h. Inclusion in company advertisements
i. Participation with management in the broad planning of professional work, assessment of work of lower level professionals, and evaluation of lower professional's performance
j. Inclusion of position and name on company/department organization charts.
k. Extension of special parking priviledges, if any.

SHOULD THE SAME FORMULA APPLY TO BOTH THE PROFESSIONAL AND THE MANAGER AND WHY?

Any sizable organization to be successful should have a single well-defined compensation program. It should be based upon the company's established policy to pay salaries equal to or above prevailing salary levels of competitive organizations. Positions should be slotted within a salary structure. Promotional and merit increase features should be incorporated that respond to economic forces both within and without the company. Both management and professional positions should be included within this single program. If this is done, the same "formula" would apply to both managers and professionals, although pay levels would not necessarily be the same across all functional lines.

HOW HIGH MAY THE PROFESSIONAL CONCEIVABLY GO IN HIS FIRM AS COMPARED WITH THE MANAGER?

It seems highly doubtful that compensation for the highest job on the professional ladder would reach the level of the executive who reports to someone at the board level of a company. The rare case of a Keyes, Edison or Steinmetz referred to in general previously could, of course, be the exception. It seems unlikely that a normally established professional ladder would reach higher than the manager responsible for incumbents in the highest professional position. It would seem unusual to pay more money to the professional than to the manager who has the ultimate responsibility for the professional's work, although there may be unusual circumstances to justify this. It is conceivable that the top professional ladder position might be as high as the manager. The most likely approach would seem to place the highest level professional position at a slightly lower level than the manager to whom he is responsible.

SOME MISCELLANEOUS THOUGHTS

a.   Professional ladders should be well publicized within the organization and provide employees with an understanding of what differentiates one level from another.

b.   The number of steps in a professional ladder should be designed to recognize significantly different levels of work at the same time providing enough levels to demonstrate progress to employees both on an individual as well as a corporate basis. This is a difficult balance. The average professional needs three to four promotional levels. There probably needs to be two or three more levels for the outstanding professionals. The more levels the greater the possibility of employee questioning management's appointments.

c.   Those professionals who generally achieve the highest endorsement from their peers are those who climb the professional ladder and reach the highest rung early in their careers.

d.   The age old problem of using the professional ladder as a dumping ground for managers who have not measured up sufficiently or who must be moved to unblock positions to be used for management development purposes will dilute or contaminate the status of the professional environment. However, if the individuals were strong professional contributors at the time they were appointed there is a change that the undesirable impact can be overcome in time.

e.   If the professional group of employees is large enough, an organization would be well advised to establish the professional ladder and give it greatest emphasis and then build the management ladder around it. Realistically however, this is not how organizations normally develop.

f.   Recognition of employees along the professional or management ladders is generally within a different time frame of an employee's career. Managers are appointed because there is a need to have a leader. Selection is based upon good (but not a long series of difficult professional problems) work and management betting on the future of an individual's management skills. Professionals are appointed only after they have repeatedly proved themselves on a long series of difficult professional problems. Their appointments only come if management is willing (rather than having a need). This tends to make equality of ladders questionable.

g. If a professional is on the same level as the manager or supervisor, per the announced ladders, there will generally be a reluctance on the part of the professional to accept assignments and have his work criticized and reviewed by the management person at the same level.

h. Despite all that managements have done to upgrade the status of professionals in companies, it does not seem that professionals accept the equality claimed for both ladders. For the immediately above reason along with control of people, work assignments, and money the managerial ladder is generally considered the best ladder to be on.

James F. Moore
Senior Advisor
Executive Compensation
Secretary's Department
Exxon Corporation

Recommendations of George H. Foote, McKinsey & Co.:

I am glad to give you some points of view on the basic issue you raise—that is, whether managers and professionals should be compensated in fundamentally different ways.

To begin with, my experience is that most companies do not see a need for totally different compensation structures for managers and for professionals; they would argue that both kinds of job can be adequately compensated within a single framework. By "structure" I mean an orderly progression of compensation grades in which each position is assigned to a grade having a midpoint reflecting the underlying value of the position, and a minimum and maximum that help determine the pay of the individual according to his tenure and performance.

The more important problem, as many companies recognize, is to have meaningful high-level positions for those people who wish to remain professionals throughout their careers. The risk is that the professional man, particularly the R&D scientist, may be forced to take a managerial position in order to enhance his compensation. Frequently, he will have neither the aptitude nor the training for it, so that the company gains a poor manager and loses a good professional. (The few outstanding exceptions—Dr. Land at Polaroid, for example—probably "prove the rule" here.)

Companies strive to create these high-level technical positions in several ways. One approach used in R&D is to adopt a matrix form of organization involving two kinds of position. The first is that of *Project Manager*, responsible for carrying through a specific pure research, applied research or commercial development project. This position combines some general management responsibilities with the problem-solving aspects of the research function.

The second position is that of *Discipline Head*, having responsibility for expanding a basic branch of science (e.g., superconductivity) that is important to the company. Depending on the company's business and products, the requirement could be for one of the two or three top individuals in that discipline worldwide. These positions would naturally be of great value to the company and would be compensated accordingly.

Having established the managerial and professional positions that will give satisfactory career progression, there are two main factors that primarily determine how much each position will be paid:

1. *The need to pay competitively.* The pay level against a man's grade should match what other people would pay him for his services. There are enough professionals employed in industry to provide good data on the rates other companies pay for positions such as business lawyers, specialist engineers, and company treasurers. The compensation opportunities in private practice can provide a useful cross-check, though these need to be modified to allow for differing employment risks, compensation that really reflects a return on the capital invested in a partnership, and so on. For industrial scientists, even at top level, comparisons can be made with those employed in universities, in governmental agencies, and in research foundations.

2. *The need to maintain internal equity.* Each job in a company should be paid what it is worth relative to each other job. Most companies would feel that existing evaluation techniques can work equally well for both professional and managerial jobs. Using these techniques, jobs are assessed against criteria such as the potential impact of the position on company financial

performance, the complexity of the tasks assigned to it, and the professional qualifications and training needed for satisfactory performance.

Our experience in Europe throws an interesting sidelight on your question regarding the ability of a professional to be paid an amount second only to the chief executive of the company. In the United States, we observe that senior staff positions (e.g., the heads of the Finance and R&D functions) tend to get paid somewhat less than the senior line managers (i.e., heads of major business groups). In Germany, by contrast, the staff positions—and in particular the heads of R&D and Engineering—would be paid more than those in the top line management positions.

George H. Foote
Director
McKinsey & Company, Inc.

With regard to the total compensation package sought by the professional "in terms of his own specific desires and needs for fulfillment," the following list has been suggested by Mr. P.A. Van Wagenen of Allegheny Ludlum Industries.[1]

"Let's examine some of the things today's professionals are seeking:

> *First*, they want involvement, hackneyed as this expression may sound. They not only want to work on challenging and meaningful assignments but they also want a hand in determining what these assignments will be. Management by mutual goal setting may be a first step in this direction
>
> *Second*, most modern professionals demand recognition of their profession rather than just being lumped into traditional molds such as supervisor, scientist, engineer, junior executive, staff assistant, trainee, etc. Discipline is a distinct source of pride to many as the rapid growth of national professional societies indicates.
>
> *Third*, the professional not only wants job challenge but a change to participate in meaningful assignments quickly. Today's exempt employee has no desire for the long and traditional 'apprentice period.' If you don't let them assume responsibility rapidly, they

may decide to try another company or situation. And remember, the cost of replacement is usually higher than the cost of retention.

Fourth, they tend to look upon promotions and salary recognition as an earned right not as a reward given them as the result of some mechanistic organization or salary administration system--which they don't agree with and may not understand or care to understand.

Fifth, today's professionals expect to be accepted completely as a member of the 'management, business or technical team' once they have proven their ability-- impatience is one of their most obvious traits. And this impatience, as you know, does not always 'sit well' with some of the traditionalists in the industrial hierarchy.

Sixth, these people expect more liberal and less structured work routines including more flexible working hours, time off (with pay) and similar 'perquisites.' And, of course, most of them take for granted that the company will provide modern facilities, equipment, support personnel, and adequate budgets.

And, finally, this volatile work group wants credit when and where credit is due. If their work is good they expect the boss will say so--not only to them but to higher management. They will not tolerate a superior who does little, if any, of the work but who takes most or all the credit."

NOTES

[1]From a speech presented to the Allegheny-Kiski Personnel Association on January 4, 1971.

BIBLIOGRAPHY

BOOKS

Anderson, Charles Edward. *Office Incentive Systems.* Waterford, Conn.: Prentice-Hall, 1964.

Ansoff, H. Igor. *Corporate Strategy.* New York: McGraw-Hill, 1965.

Arensberg, Conrod M. (et al.), ed. *Research in Industrial Human Relations.* New York: Harper & Bros., 1957.

Argyris, Chris. *Integrating the Individual and the Organization.* New York: John Wiley & Sons, Inc., 1964.

_____. *Management and Organizational Development.* New York: McGraw-Hill, 1971.

_____. *Organization and Innovation.* Homewood, Ill.: Richard D. Irwin, 1965.

_____. *Personality and Organization; The Conflict Between System and the Individual.* New York: Harper & Bros., 1957.

_____. *Understanding Organizational Behavior.* Homewood, Ill.: Dorsey Press, 1960.

Bacon, Jeremy. *Executive Compensation Plans in the Smaller Company.* New York: National Industrial Conference Board, 1970.

Beach, Dale S. *Managing People at Work (Readings).* New York: Macmillan Co., 1971.

Becker, Ester. *Dictionary of Personnel and Industrial Relations.* New York: Philosophical Library, Inc. 1958.

Belcher, David W. *Wage and Salary Administration.* 2nd ed. Englewood Cliffs, N.J.: Prentice-Hall, 1962.

Bellamy, Edward. *Looking Backward: 2000-1887.* Cleveland: World Publishing Co., 1950.

Bennis, Warren G. *Changing Organizations.* New York: McGraw-Hill, 1966.

_____. *Interpersonal Dynamics.* Homewood, Ill.: Dorsey Press, 1964.

_____. *Organizational Concepts and Analysis,* edited by Edward G. Scott. Belmont, Calif.: Dickerson Publ. Co., 1969.

Boguslaw, Robert. *The New Utopians, A Study of System Design and Social Change.* Englewood Cliffs, N.J.: Prentice-Hall, 1965.

Brennan, Charles W. *Wage Administration*, rev. ed. Homewood, Ill.:   Richard D. Irwin, 1963.

Bright, James R., ed. *Research, Development and Technological Innovation.* Homewood, Ill.:   Richard D. Irwin, 1964.

_____. *Technological Forecasting for Industry and Management.* Englewood Cliffs, N.J.: Prentice-Hall, 1968.

Brown, E. H. Phelps, and Browne, Margaret. *A Century of Pay.* New York: St. Martin's Press, 1968.

Brown, Harrison, and Weir, John. *The Next Hundred Years.* New York: Viking Press, 1957.

Burgess, Leonard R. *Top Executive Pay Package.*   New York: Free Press, 1963.

_____. *Wage and Salary Administration in a Dynamic Economy.* New York: Harcourt, Brace & World, Inc., 1968.

Burke, J.G. *The New Technology and Human Values.*   Belmont, Calif.:   Wadsworth Publishing Co., 1966.

Burnham, James. *The Theory of the Managerial Revolution.* New York: John Day Co., Inc., 1941.

Burns, Eveline Mabel.   *Wages and the State.* London: P. S. King & Son Ltd., 1926.

Campbell, John Paul; Donnette, M.D.; Lawler, E.E.; and Weick, K.E. *Managerial Behavior, Performance, and Effectiveness.* New York: McGraw-Hill, 1970.

Cartter, Allan Murray. *Theory of Wages and Employment.* Homewood, Ill.:   Richard D. Irwin, 1959.

Cartter, Allan Murray, and Marshall, R. F. *Labor Economics: Wages, Employment and Trade Unionism.*   Homewood, Ill.:   Richard D. Irwin, 1967.

Cetron, Marvin J. *Technical Resource Management.*   Cambridge, Mass.:   M.I.T. Press, 1969.

Chamberlain, Neil W. Quoted by Don Fabon in *The Dynamics of Change.* Englewood Cliffs: Prentice-Hall, 1968.

Chernick, Jack, and Hellickson, George C. *Guaranteed Annual Wages.* Minneapolis: U. of Minn. Press, 1945.

Chruden, Herbert J., and Sherman, Arthur W., Jr. Personnel *Management.* 4th ed. Cincinnati: South-Western Publ. Co., 1973.

Clark, John Bates. *Distribution of Wealth.*   New York: Macmillan Co., 1899.

Clarke, A.C. *The Profiles of the Future.* New York: Harper & Row, 1962.

Cofer, Charles Norval, and Appley, M. H. *Motivation: Theory and Research.* New York: John Wiley & Sons, 1964.

Copeland, Melvin Thomas. *The Executive at Work.* Cambridge, Mass.: Harvard Univ. Press, 1951.

Dale, Ernest. *Management: Theory and Practice.* New York: McGraw-Hill, 1965.

_____. *Readings in Management; Landmarks and New Frontiers.* New York: McGraw-Hill, 1970.

Danielson, Lee E. *Characteristics of Engineers and Scientists, Report No. 11.* Ann Arbor: U. of Mich., 1960.

Davidson, John. *The Bargaining Theory of Wages.* New York: G. P. Putnam's Sons, 1898.

Davis, Keith. *Human Behavior at Work.* New York: McGraw-Hill, 1972.

_____. *Human Relations at Work.* New York: McGraw-Hill, 1967.

de Jouvenel, Bertrand. *The Art of Conjecture.* New York: Basic Books, 1966.

Deric, Arthur J., ed. *The Total Approach to Employee Benefits.* New York: Amer. Management Assoc., 1967.

Dickson, William John, and Roethlisberger, F. J. *Counseling in an Organization.* Boston: Harvard Univ., 1966.

Diebold, John. *Beyond Automation.* New York: McGraw-Hill, 1964.

Drucker, Peter Ferdinand. *The Age of Discontinuity.* New York: Harper & Row, 1969.

_____. *The New Society.* New York: Harper & Row, 1949.

_____. *Preparing Tomorrow's Business Leaders Today.* Englewood Cliffs, N.J.: Prentice-Hall, 1969.

Dubin, Robert. *World at Work.* Englewood Cliffs, N.J.: Prentice-Hall, 1958.

_____. ed. *Handbook of Work, Organization and Society.* Chicago: Rand McNally, 1968.

Dunlop, John T., ed. *Theory of Wage Determination.* New York: St. Martin's Press, 1957.

Dunn, J. D., and Rachel, Frank M. *Wage and Salary Administration: Total Compensation Systems.* New York: McGraw-Hill, 1971.

Ewing, David W., and Fenn, Dan H., eds. *Incentives for Executives.* New York: McGraw-Hill, 1962.

Fabun, Don. *The Dynamics of Change.* Englewood Cliffs, N.J.: Prentice-Hall, 1968.

Farmer, Richard N. *Management in the Future.* Belmont, Calif.: Wadsworth Publ. Co., 1967.

Fayol, Henri. *General and Industrial Management.* London: Sir Isaac Pitman & Sons, 1949.

Ferguson, Robert H. *Wages, Earnings, and Incomes: Definitions of Terms and Sources of Data.* Ithaca, N.Y.: Cornell Univ., 1971.

Fetter, Robert B., and Johnson, Donald C. *Compensation and Incentives for Industrial Executives.* Bloomington, Ind.: Indiana U. Press, 1952.

Flippo, Edwin B. *Management: A Behavioral Approach.* Boston: Allyn & Bacon, 1966.

_____. *Profit Sharing in American Business.* Columbus, O.: Ohio State Univ., 1954.

Follett, Mary Parker. *Freedom and Coordination.* London: Mgm't Publications Trust Ltd., 1949.

Ford, Henry. *My Life and Work.* New York: Doubleday, Page & Co., 1924.

Friedman, Milton. *Capitalism and Freedom.* Chicago: Univ. of Chicago Press, 1962.

Fuller, Don. *Manage or be Managed.* Boston: Farnsworth Publ. Co., 1964.

Gabor, Denis. *Inventing the Future.* New York: Alfred A. Knopf, 1964.

Gardner, John W. *Excellence.* New York: Harper & Row, 1962.

_____. *Self Renewal: The Individual and the Innovative Society.* New York: Harper & Row, 1964.

Gellerman, Saul. *Management by Motivation.* New York: Amer. Management Assoc., 1968.

_____. *Motivating Men with Money.* New York: Amer. Management Assoc., 1965.

_____. *Motivation and Productivity.* New York: Amer. Management Assoc., 1963.

_____. *People, Problems and Profits.* New York: McGraw-Hill, 1960.

Gray, Robert D. *Frontiers in Industrial Relations.* Pasadena: Cal Tech, 1959.

Greene, Mark R. *The Role of Employee Benefit Structurees in Manufacturing Industry.* Eugene, Oregon: The Univ. of Oregon, 1964.

Haimann, Theodore. *Professional Management: Theory and Practice.*   Boston: Houghton Mifflin Co., 1962.

_____.   and Scott, William G. *Management in the Modern Organization.*   Boston: Houghton Mifflin Co., 1970.

Haire, Mason. *Psychology in Management.* 2nd ed.   New York: McGraw-Hill, 1964.

Hampton, David R.   *Behavioral Concepts in Management.*   2nd ed. Belmont, Calif.: Dickerson Publ. Co., 1972.

_____.   *Modern Management: Issues and Ideas.*   Belmont, Calif.:   Dickerson Publ. Co., 1969.

Helmer, Olaf.   *Social Technology.* New York: Basic Books, 1966.

Heneman, H. G., Jr., and Yoder, Dale.   *Labor Economics.* Cincinnati: South-Western Publ. Co., 1965.

Heneman, H. G. (et al.).   *Employment Relations Research.*   New York: Harper & Bros., 1960.

Herzberg, Frederick, and Mausner, Bernard.   *The Motivation to Work.* 2nd ed.   New York: John Wiley & Sons Inc., 1959.

Herzberg, Frederick (et al.).   *Job Attitudes: Review of Research and Opinion.* Pittsburgh: Psychological Services of Pittsburgh, 1957.

_____.   *Work and Nature of Man.*   New York: World Publ. Co., 1966.

Hick, Herbert C., and Gullett, C. Ray.   *Modern Business Management.*   New York: McGraw-Hill, 1974.

Hinrichs, J.R.   *High-Talent Personnel: Managing a Critical Resource.*   New York: Amer. Management Assoc., 1966.

Huan-Chang, C. "Economic Principles in Ancient China--As Confucius Saith."   *In The World of Business,* edited by E. C. Burck, e al.   New York: Simon & Schuster, 1962.

Indik, Bernard P.   *The Motivation to Work.*   New Brunswick, N. J. :   Rutgers Univ., 1966.

Jaques, Elliott.   *Equitable Payment.*   New York: John Wiley & Sons Inc., 1961.

_____.   *Measurement of Responsibility: A Study of Work, Payment, and Individual Capacity.*   Cambridge, Mass.:   Harvard Univ. Press, 1956.

_____.   *Time-Span Handbook*   London: Heinemann, 1964.

Jehring, John James. *Increased Incentives through Profit Sharing.* Evanston, Ill.: Profit Sharing Research Foundation, 1960.

_____, and Voelker, K. E. *Office Incentives.* Madison: U. of Wis., 1964.

Jennings, Eugene. *Executive Success.* New York: Appleton-Century-Crofts, 1967.

_____. *The Executive.* New York: Harper & Row, 1962.

_____. *The Mobile Manager.*

Jucius, M. J. *Personnel Management.* 5th ed. Homewood, Ill.: Richard D. Irwin, 1963.

_____, and Schlender, William E. *Elements of Managerial Action.* Homewood, Ill.: Richard D. Irwin, 1965.

Kahn, Herman, and Wiener, Anthony J. *The Year 2000: A Framework for Speculation on the Next 33 Years.* New York: Macmillan Co., 1967.

Kaplan, A. D. H. *The Guarantee of Annual Wages.* Washington, D. C.: The Brookings Institute, 1947.

Kerr, Clark; Dunlop, John T.; Harbison, Frederick H.; and Myers, Charles A. *Industrialism and Industrial Man.* Cambridge, Mass.: Harvard Univ. Press, 1960.

Keynes, John Maynard. *The General Theory of Employment, Interest, and Money.* New York: Harcourt, Brace & Co., 1936.

Knowlton, P. A. *Profit Sharing Patterns.* Evanston, Ill.: Profit Sharing Research Foundations, 1954.

Koontz, Harold, and O'Donnell, Cyril. *Appraising Managers as Managers.* New York: McGraw-Hill, 1971.

_____. *Principles of Management.* New York: McGraw-Hill, 1968.

Lanham, Elizabeth. *Administration of Wages and Salaries.* New York: Harper & Row, 1963.

Lauterbach, Albert T. *Man, Motives, and Money; Psychological Frontiers of Economics.* Ithaca, N.Y.: Cornell Univ. Press, 1954.

Lawler, Edward E. *Pay and Organizational Effectiveness: A Psychological View.* New York: McGraw-Hill, 1971.

Leftwich, Richard H. *The Price System and Resource Allocation.* 3rd ed. New York: Holt, Rinehart & Winston, 1966.

Lewellen, W. G. *Executive Compensation in Large Industrial Organizations.* New York: National Bureau of Economic Research, 1968.

Lincoln, James F. *Incentive Management.* Cleveland: Lincoln Electric Co., 1951.

____. *Lincoln's Incentive System.* New York: McGraw-Hill, 1946.

Lipset, Seymour Martin, and Bendix, Reinhard. *Social Mobility in Industrial Society.* Berkeley: Univ. of California Press, 1959.

Lovejoy, Lawrence C. *Wage and Salary Administration.* New York: Ronald Press, 1959.

McClelland, David C. *The Achieving Society.* Princeton, N.J.: Van Nostrand, 1961.

____, and Winter, D. G. *The Achievement Motive.* New York: Appleton-Century-Crofts, 1953.

____. *Human Motivation.* Morristown, N.J.: General Learning Press, 1973.

____. *Motivating Economic Achievement.* New York: Free Press, 1969.

McConnell, Campbell R. *Perspectives on Wage Determination.* New York: McGraw-Hill, 1970.

McFarland, Dalton E. *Management: Principles and Practices.* New York: Macmillan Co., 1964.

McGregor, Douglas. *The Human Side of Enterprise.* New York: McGraw-Hill, 1960.

____. *Leadership and Motivation.* Cambridge, Mass.: M.I.T. Press, 1966.

McQuaig, J. H. *How to Motivate Men.* New York: Frederick Fell, Inc., 1967.

Mann, R., ed. *The Arts of Top Management: A McKinsey Anthology.* New York: McGraw-Hill, 1971.

March, James G., ed. *Handbook of Organizations.* Chicago: Rand McNally & Co., 1965.

Marrow, Alfred J. *Making Management Human.* New York: McGraw-Hill, 1957.

Maslow, Abraham Harold. *Motivation and Personality.* New York: Harper & Bros., 1954.

Maule, Frances. *Executive Careers for Women.* New York: Harper & Bros., 1961.

Mee, John F. *Management Thought in a Dynamic Economy.* New York: N.Y. Univ. Press, 1963.

Merrett, A. J., and White, M. R. M. *Incentive Payment Systems for Managers.* London: Gower Press Ltd., 1968.

Mescon, Michael H. (et al.). *The Management of Enterprise.* New York: Macmillan, 1973.

_____. *The Problems of Businessmen.* Atlanta: Georgia State College, 1965.

Metzger, Bertram L. *Indexed Bibliography on Profit-Sharing. 1940-1958.* Evanston, Ill.: Profit Sharing Research Foundation, 1959.

_____. *Profit Sharing in Perspective.* 2nd ed. Evanston, Ill.: Profit Sharing Research Foundation, 1966.

Miner, John B. *The Management Process, Theory, Research, and Practice.* New York: Macmillan Co., 1973.

_____. *Management Theory.* New York: Macmillan Co., 1971.

_____, and Miner, Mary Green. *Personnel and Industrial Relations.* 2nd ed. New York: Macmillan Co., 1973.

Miner, John B., and Nash, Allan N. *Personnel and Labor Relations.* New York: Macmillan Co., 1973.

Moore, Franklin G., ed. *A Management Sourcebook.* New York: Harper & Row, 1964.

Moore, Russell Franklin, ed. *Compensating Executive Worth.* New York: Amer. Management Assoc., 1968.

Orwell, George. *Nineteen Eighty-four.* New York: Harcourt & Brace & Co., 1949.

Patton, Arch. *What is an Executive Worth?* New York: McGraw-Hill, 1961.

Pfiffner, J. M., and Sherwood, F. P. *Administrative Organization.* Englewood Cliffs, N. J.: Prentice-Hall, 1960.

Pigors, Paul, and Malm, F. T., eds. *Management of Human Resources.* New York: McGraw-Hill, 1969.

Pigors, Paul, and Myers, Charles A. *Personnel Administration.* New York: McGraw-Hill, 1969.

Prehoda, R.W. *Designing the Future: The Role of Technological Forecasting.* Philadelphia: Chilton Book Co., 1967.

Rand, Ayn. *Atlas Shrugged.* New York: Random House, 1957.

_____. *The Fountainhead.* Indianapolis, N. Y.: The Bobbs-Merrill Co., 1943.

Reid, Graham L., and Robertson, D. J. *Fringe Benefits, Labor Costs and Social Security.* London: George Allen & Unwin Ltd., 1965.

Reisman, David (et al.). *The Lonely Crowd.* New Haven: Yale Univ. Press, 1950.

Richards, M.D., and Nielander, W. A., eds. *Readings in Management.* 2nd ed. Cincinnati: South-Western Publ. Co., 1963.

Riegel, John Wallace. *Administration of Salaries for Engineers and Scientists.* Ann Arbor: U. of Michigan, 1958.

_____. *Intangible Rewards for Engineers and Scientists.* Ann Arbor: U. of Michigan, 1958.

Sargent, Charles W. *"Fringe" Benefits: Do We Know Enough About Them?* Hanover, N.H.: Dartmouth College, 1953.

Sayles, Leonard R. *Individualism and Big Business.* New York: McGraw-Hill, 1963.

Schwartz, P. *Attitudes of Middle Management Personnel.* Pittsburgh: American Institute for Research, 1959.

Servan-Schreiber, J. J. *The American Challenge.* New York: Atheneum House, 1968.

Sibson, Robert Earl. *Wages and Salaries: A Handbook for Line Managers* (rev. ed.). New York: Amer. Management Assoc., 1967.

Sisk, Henry L. *Management and Organization.* 2nd ed. Cincinnati: South-Western Publ. Co., 1973.

Slichter, S. H. (et al). *The Impact of Collective Bargaining on Management.* Washington: Brookings Institute, 1960.

Smith, Adam. *An Inquiry into the Nature and Causes of Wealth of Nations.* Scotland: Adam & Chas. Black, 1863.

Smyth, Richard C. *Financial Incentives for Management.* New York: McGraw-Hill, 1960.

Snider, Joseph L. *The Guarantee of Work and Wages.* Boston: Harvard Univ. Grad. Schl. of Bus., 1947.

Somers, Herman M., and Somers, Anne R. *Doctors, Patients, and Health Insurance.* Washington: Brookings Institute, 1961.

Stagner, Ross. *Psychology of Industrial Conflict.* New York: John Wiley & Sons, 1956.

Steiner, George Albert. *Top Management Planning.* New York: Macmillan Co., 1969.

Suojanen, Waino W. *The Dynamics of Management.* New York: Holt, Rinehart and Winston, 1966.

Taylor, George William. *Government Regulation of Industrial Relations.* Englewood Cliffs, N.J.: Prentice-Hall, 1948.

___, and Pierson, Frank C., ed. *New Concepts in Wage Determination.* New York: McGraw-Hill, 1957.

Terry, G. R. *Principles of Management.* 4th ed. Homewood, Ill.: Richard D. Irwin, 1964.

Thibaut, John W., and Kelley, Harold H. *The Social Psychology of Groups.* New York: John Wiley & Sons, 1966.

Thomson, Sir George Paget. *The Foreseeable Future.* London: Readers Union Cambridge Univ. Press, 1957.

Thorndike, R. L. *Personnel Selection.* New York: John Wiley & Sons Inc., 1949.

Tiffin, J., and McCormick, E. J. *Industrial Psychology.* 5th ed. Englewood Cliffs, N.J.:; Prentice-Hall, 1965.

Toffler, Alvin. *Future Shock.* New York: Random House, 1970.

Tugwell, Rexford Guy. *The Industrial Discipline.* New York: Columbia Press, 1933.

Vroom, Victor Harold. *Work and Motivation.* New York: John Wiley & Sons Inc., 1964.

Washington, George Thomas, and Rothschild, V. Henry II. *Compensating the Corporate Executive.* New York: Ronald Press, 1962.

Weber, Max. *The Protestant Ethic and the Spirit of Capitalism.* New York: Charles Scribner's Sons, 1958.

Whyte, William Foote (et al.) *Money and Motivation.* New York: Harper & Bros., 1955.

Whyte, W. H., Jr. *The Organization Man.* New York: Simon & Schuster, 1958.

Wickert, Frederic R., and McFarland, Dalton E. *Measuring Executive Effectiveness.* New York: Appleton-Century-Crofts, 1967.

Wootton, Barbara. *The Social Foundation of Wage Policy.* London: Allen & Unwin, 1955.

Zollitsch, Herbert G., and Langsner, Adolph. *Wage and Salary Administration.* 2nd ed. Cincinnati: South-Western Publ. Co., 1970.

INDEX

Administrative personnel, defined, 8
Agriculture Department. *See* U.S. Department of Agriculture
American Compensation Association, 10
American Management Association, 1
Aristotle, 19
Attitudes: in appraising managerial success, 38; of professionals turned manager, 43-44
Attorneys. *See* Lawyers
Authority and responsibility: exercise of as compensation, 7; of managers, 35-37; in determining compensation levels, 41-42, 100; of professionals, 106-107
Automation, Marxian basis for opposition to, 20
Automobile industry, double-track compensation system in, 94
Awards and prizes as compensation, 7, 28, 29

Bargaining Theory of Wages, 23-24; influences affecting, 24-28
Belcher, David W., 1, 2, 29, 30
Bonuses: 1, 7, 28, 29; in the Productive Efficiency theory of wages, 23
Building materials industry, double-track compensation system in, 95
Business management. *See* Management

Chapman, John F., 29
Chemical industry, double-track compensation system in, 75
Civil Service System, 48
Clark, John Bates, 23
Classical theory of wages. *See* "Social" wage theories
Clausen, A. W., 36
Clay industries, double-track compensation systems in, 75
Collective bargaining: in the Bargaining Theory of Wages, 24; in Institutional Wage theory, 22; in the Neo-Keynesian Distribution theory of wages, 21
Communication skills, in determining manager compensation, 101
Compensation. *See* Employee compensation; Total compensation

Concrete industry, double-track compensation system in, 75
Conditions of labor, 7
Conference Board, 1, 28
Consumption, high wages as a means of increasing, 21
Consumption theory of wages, 21
Corporate size, use of double-track compensation systems and, 10, 74-75, 86
Creativity, opportunity for as compensation, 7

Data processing/systems departments, double-track compensation systems in, 76, 77
Davidson, John, 23
Decision-making: by professionals who have become managers, 48; as a factor in managerial compensation, 40, 41
Dentists, compensation for, 3
DeYoung, Russell, 36
Doctors. *See* Physicians
Double-track system of compensation and progression. *See* Employee compensation
Drug trade. *See* Pharmaceutical industry

Education of workers: as a function of compensation, 85; in the Investment theory of wages, 21. *See also* Employee training
Electric and electronic machinery industry, double-track compensation system in, 75, 95
Ellig, Bruce R., 80
Emotional stability, in determining manager compensation, 100. *See also* Job stress
Employee compensation: background to, 1-2; categories of factors in, 28-32; double-track compensation and progression system, 2, 4, 7; conclusions regarding, 69-82; advancement levels in, 76, 78-80; departmental use of, 76, 77; experts in the field of, 80-81; future use of, 80; percentage of firms using, 70-74; corporate size and, 10; defined, 9; factors to consider in establishing, 99-106; implications of, 83-90; advantages of utilizing, 83-86;